T0078421

The Council of God
Murder or Self Defense?

By

Leon Davis
B.A. Southern University, 1972

Thesis submitted to the faculty of the Graduate School
Of Northwestern State University of Louisiana
In partial fulfillment of the requirements for the degree of
Master of Arts

authorHOUSE°

AuthorHouse™
1663 Liberty Drive
Bloomington, IN 47403
www.authorhouse.com
Phone: 833-262-8899

© 2020 Leon Davis. All rights reserved.

No part of this book may be reproduced, stored in a retrieval system, or
transmitted by any means without the written permission of the author.

Published by AuthorHouse 11/25/2020

ISBN: 978-1-6655-0864-3 (sc)
ISBN: 978-1-6655-0863-6 (e)

Print information available on the last page.

Any people depicted in stock imagery provided by Getty Images are models,
and such images are being used for illustrative purposes only.
Certain stock imagery © Getty Images.

This book is printed on acid-free paper.

Because of the dynamic nature of the Internet, any web addresses or
links contained in this book may have changed since publication and may
no longer be valid. The views expressed in this work are solely those
of the author and do not necessarily reflect the views of the publisher,
and the publisher hereby disclaims any responsibility for them.

CIRCULATION AGREEMENT

In presenting this thesis for an advanced degree at Northwestern State University, I agree that the library of the University shall make it available for inspection and circulation in accordance with its regulations governing materials of this type. I further agree that permission to copy from, or to publish, this thesis may be granted by the professor under whose direction it was written or, in his absence, by the Dean of the Graduate School when such copying or publication is intended solely for the purpose of scholarly research and does not involve financial gain. It is understood that any copying from, or publication of, this thesis, which involves potential financial gain will not be allowed without written permission from the author. Copyright 2002 by Leon W. Davis. All rights reserved.

_____

Leon W. Davis

NOTICE TO BORROWERS

Unpublished thesis deposited in the Northwestern State University Library must be used only in accordance with the stipulations prescribed by the author in the preceding statement.

The author of this thesis is :

Leon W. Davis
804 Lou Street
Natchitoches, Louisiana 71457

The director of this thesis is:

Dr. James McCorkle
Department of Social Sciences
Northwestern State University
Natchitoches, Louisiana 71457

Users of this thesis not regularly enrolled as students at Northwesertern State University are required to attest acceptance of the preceding stipulations by signing below.

Libraries borrowing this thesis for the use of their patrons are required to see that each user records here, the information requested.

NAME OF USER	ADDRESS	DATE	TYPE OF USE

ACKNOWLEDGEMENTS

Many thanks are appropriate to the people who helped make this thesis possible. Mainly, I would like to thank my graduate committee who deserves sincere thanks for reading, editing and improving the quality of this paper. My very heart felt gratitude to Dr. James McCorkle, Dr.Marietta LeBreton and Dr. Brenden Martin. Dr. B. Martin and Dr. Jeffrey Smith who encourage me with the vision to complete a thesis paper instead of a paper in lieu of thesis. Thank you for your insight.

I would also like to thank Mrs. Mary Linn Wernet and others of the Cammie G. Henry Research Center and the Watson Library Staff who I also solicited at Northwestern State University who were of utmost assistance in my search for the material that was the foundation for this thesis.

Many thanks to my brother, Gary W. Davis for his important insight in my Endeavor. My sister, Rhonda Braden and her son, Tommy for doing most of the final typing for this thesis.

Lastly, I would like to thank the staff of Tulane University Armistad Center and the people at the University of New Orleans. My special thanks goes out to the librarian at the Orleans Parish Library at New Orleans for helping me research the exact records of the courts involved in this thesis.

Finally to the reader, I wish to acknowledge that any and all errors found within this work are the sole responsibility of the author.

TABLE OF CONTENTS

Illustrations

1. A picture of the Council of God as the Black Hand.

2. A Picture of Jack Pierre on the right and Edward Honore on the left. Both leaders of the Council of God.

3. A picture of the Council of God members being held in jail.

4. The House where the incident occurred.

JACK PIERRE AND EDWARD HONORE,
Council of God Negroes, Who Will Be Hanged To-Day.

A GROUP OF PRISONERS.

(Photo by J. de B. Seguin.)

Joseph Gasner, Thomas Mason, Severin Zenion, Marie Honoré, Robert Daniel, Jacques Pierre, Dennis Latimore.

ABSTRACT

Leon W. Davis, B.S., Southern University, 1972.

Master of Arts, Northwestern State University, Fall Commencement, 2002.

Major: American History/Afro American History

"The Council of God: Murder or Self-Defense.

Thesis directed by Professor James McCorkle

Pages in thesis, 105. Words in abstract, 209.

The plight of Negroes in the City of New Orleans in 1907 were reflections of the Negroes during the Nadir of Blacks in America. The years of reconstruction had produced in New Orleans the existence of a state of segregation and the lack of political power by Black Americans which made the conditions that created the incident called the Council of God incident.

Robert Charles in 1900 created a fear of Blacks who possessed self-identity other than that ascribed to Negroes in Louisiana. Robert Charles was the recipient of fierce hatred for those Negroes who dared to defend themselves from Anglo-American mobs during the Nadir, 1890-1910. The Council of God was only of those organizations created in a religious fervor and determines to reinterpret the role of religion in an attempt to gain freedom.

The Council of God incident began with the death of Robert Cambias a New Orleans policeman. The drama was played out in the Courts of New Orleans and the State Supreme Court of Louisiana. Both leaders of the new religion were tried for Robert Cambias death. They were tried and found guilty of murdering a white policeman. They were hanged for the murder of Mr. Cambias.

But they were not guilty of murder but acted in self-defense.

INTRODUCTION

The Council of God: Murder or Self-Defense?

On Friday, October 18, 1907, an incident of racial violence occurred in New Orleans, Louisiana, reflected the "white South" brutal repression of a black self-defense movement. The Council of God was a religious movement in New Orleans in the early 1900s that advocated self-defense and had organized the Black Community. The council believed that white hatred for the Negro was inspired by the fact that Black men did not pray to him but to the God who wrote the Ten Commandments. According to their beliefs, the Negro was the true Israelite, the real Jew in whom all promises are fulfilled. Circumcision was one of the cult's basic practices.

The prophet claimed that Christ had done this so they, his followers, should do likewise. The Negro's birthright had been taken from him by those people professing to be Jews, who bought the name from the Pope of Rome at a time when he ruled the world. They claimed that the Black man labored under the curse of slavery because the Pope subjected and killed Christ.

The incident occurred when some boys were throwing rocks at a building in which the Council of God was meeting. Some of the members came outside to see who was throwing rocks on the building. They came across John Sherman whom they apprehended as the culprit. John Sherman stated that one of the members cut him. He was able to free himself and run to get the police.

Officer Robert Cambias was on duty that night near the area where the incident had occurred. John Sherman told Officer Cambias that some black men had attacked him.

When Officer Robert Cambias awoke that day, he dreamed about being hurt by some evil force. Officer Cambias now proceeded with John Sherman to find the assailants. The Council of God had returned to its meeting when Officer Cambias knocked on the door. The head butler, who was an important member of the group, met him. It was his house where the meeting was being held. Officer Cambias then proceeded to arrest some of the members, although he had no warrant or evidence as to which individual committed the offense. He told them that he was going to arrest someone even if it killed him. He and some of the members began to argue and the officer pulled his gun and one of the members grabbed him. In the scuffle, Officer Cambias was killed with a knife. John Sherman ran to report what had happened. More police arrived later to retrieve Officer Robert Cambias' body. They also came to arrest the perpetrator of the hideous crime.

There was a confrontation with the whole police force. Two members of the Council of God were killed. One other officer was killed and one was wounded. After the gun battle, the house was set on fire to bring out the resisting offenders. The members of the Council were arrested and taken to jail.

The Council's members were indicted for murder. Two of the members were charged with the death of Officer Cambias. Edward Honore and Jack Pierre were tried for the murder of the officer. The trial was held two months later. Honore and Pierre plead innocent, but the district attorney obtained a conviction. The testimony of the Council members was used to convict Honore and Pierre. Both men appealed to the Louisiana Supreme Court, but lost their appeals and were sentenced to be hanged. Over two hundred people attended the hanging. It was social outing for the white community. Honore and Pierre were hung by the neck until they were dead.

This thesis will be guided by four questions. The first, was the Council of God a victim of media hysteria? The Daily Picayune was foremost in convicting the members of the Council of God by bias reporting before the trial. The papers mounted a campaign of slander and prejudice that set the stage for a conviction. The second question was did the Council of God act in self-defense when they were attacked by the police, and did Honore and Pierre merely defend themselves when officer Cambias pulled his gun? The third question, was the Council of God a Christian movement that did not advocate the forgiveness tenets of the New Testament? This organization believed in self-defense. It was an early manifestation of the Black consciousness movement.

Unlike most Black religious movements, this movement was not handicapped by the use of the forgiveness sentiments of Jesus. The Fourth question, was the Council of God the creation of Blacks that adopted the views of the Old Testament? They gave themselves titles that were found in the Old Testament. They proclaimed that they were the true Israelites. This was a departure from the philosophy of other Baptist or Christian churches in the Black community. The Council of God had tenets similar to the Black Christian nationalist movement of the 1960's. The Black Christian nationalist movement was founded by Revered Albert Cleage in the 1960's.

The belief in a Black God was one of these tenets. The Black Christian nationalist movement was founded by Revered Albert Cleage in the 1960's.

BACKGROUND

THE EARLY CHURCH

The years preceding 1907 was a time of growth for Negro preachers. The whites had suppressed the religion of Africans in America. Africans were not allowed to practice their traditional religions thus creating a vacuum in the African life where religion was a part of all social and political institutions. The value that all men are created in the image of the creator sustains all other belief systems that permeated the African psyche. Once Africans were taught that God and Jesus were white, thus destroying African spiritual conceptions of one Creator, the white slave master had created the vehicle for black self-hate. This also called forth an inferiority complex that remained in the psyche of blacks. This white superiority has been promoted through religion, politics and the cultural destruction of African self-identity. The Black Church in America is an adaptation of foreign institutions that the African seized to rebuild his humanity.

The Black Church experience in America has filled the vacuum of the African religious approach to life altered during submergence of African culture in America. The Black Church was a protest movement during slavery. It had the potential to be a black power movement in the slave community. The church in the black community has had the mission of promoting the eschatological recognition that freedom and equality are the essence of humanity. This also brought forth the idea that slavery and segregation

1

were not compatible to Christianity. Freedom was the theme of the black church during slavery. It created an avenue for protest and action in the black man's liberation.[1]

The liberation tradition of the black church was related to the fight of blacks to achieve liberation by any means necessary. The idea that God supported blacks in their rebellion against slavery even included the use of violence to achieve liberation from American slavery. The black interpretation of the Bible as an instrument in their struggle against injustice was compared to His deliverance of the Nation of Israel from Egyptian slavery and their liberation from the white institution in America. The Council of God (a religious group in New Orleans, 1907) saw the Old Testament stories of Exodus, the prophets and the New Testament apocalypse as signs of God's hope for their freedom. They believed that slavery was inconsistent with the Will of God. The three largest slave revolts in American history were planned and led by slave preachers: Gabriel Prosser in 1800 near Richmond; Denmark Vessey in 1822 in Charleston. Both failed because of betrayal. Nat Turner's bloody insurrection in 1831 in South Hampton only partially succeeded. These uprisings seemed to deny that the slaves were satisfied and content with their conditions. The leaders of these revolts used religious gatherings such as church meetings, prayer meetings and church worship time for the planning of revolts.[2]

---

[1] John Brown Childs, The Black Political Minister (Boston: G. K. Hall and Co.., 1908), 15.
[2] C. Eric Lincoln, The Black Church in the African American Experience (Durham: Duke University Press, 1990), 203.

The religion of blacks in America exemplified the kinds of political and economic institution promoted by its leaders. The religion of blacks with a nationalist interpretation comes from the leaders that promote black power. Black political and economic movements are interwoven in the black religious sentiments. Henry Highland Garnet was a pre-civil war Black Presbyterian minister who urged the slaves of the South to kill the white master that would not liberate them. Garnet is considered the father of Black Nationalism in America. Garnet also exposed the glory of Africa by discovering the great civilizations in Africa. These ideas are contrasted with the early ideas of Frederick Douglas, an integrationist/radical that cooperated with the white abolitionist William Lloyd Garrison before and during the civil war. The religious movements in the African American community reflect this Nationalist/integrationist trend in the political and economic ideas of its leaders.[3]

Black leaders have assailed the white masters since the era of freed slaves with words of condemnation. Even John Brown, a white man, who southern white Americans deemed insane, pronounced the verdict of sin on slavery in America. The admonitions of Thomas Fortune, an early 1800s leader among blacks, were ignored because after slavery and reconstruction, white America sought to dominate the black man by returning to the violence which was displayed during slavery.

> We have been robbed of the honest wages of our toil; we have been robbed of the substance of our citizenship by murder and intimidation; we have been outraged by enemies and deserted by

---

[3] John H. Bracey, et al., Black Nationalism in America (New York: Bobbs-Merril Company, Inc., 1970), 114-5.

friends; and because in a society governed by law, we have been true to the law, true to treacherous friends and as true in distrust of our enemies. It has been charged upon us that we are not made of the stern stuff which makes the Anglo Saxon race, the most consummated masters of hypocrisy, of roguery, of insolence, of arrogance and of cowardice in the history of races.[4]

The Negroes of New Orleans met the challenge of freedom with great vigor during reconstruction. The African American emerged out of slavery, with vivid memories of being under the white masters. The most telling experience of blacks during bondage was his inability to protect his wife and daughter from sexual advances of the white man. The helplessness of black slave women was shown in the white males use of her to fulfill their sexual desire. The result of this was a mulatto society of blacks in New Orleans who called themselves free people of color. New Orleans and Charleston, South Carolina produced men who were identified as black but who carried the stigma of Creoles who were of mixed parentage. During reconstruction, Creole men and women who had obtained a great deal of wealth and education were leaders in the politics of Louisiana and South Carolina.[5]

Defenders of white supremacy in New Orleans were the white owned newspapers, the New Orleans Picayune and the Time Democrat which continually vilified and ridiculed blacks. The negative terms used to identify the African Americans were "niggers", "darkies" and "sambos". White journalists portrayed the blacks as speaking an incomprehensible dialect. The African American, immoral, criminal, debased, dishonest, crazy, brutal and as a lustful

---

[4] Ibid., P. 215.

4

subhuman species. They portrayed the black man as never producing a civilization worthy of recognition.[6]

The economic system of slavery was entrenched in Louisiana and was part of the southern Black Belt. Louisiana and New Orleans were the centers of a slave holding autocracy. The contrast of white dominance and black submission, white wealth and black poverty, white education and enforced black ignorance was most vivid during the antebellum era. These areas retained white racism after the Civil War.[7] Even today the racism of this area of the south has retained the most residue of the antebellum south.

LATER DEVELOPMENT OF THE BLACK CHURCH

The dominant church of Africans in New Orleans before the Civil War was to leave the Catholic Church.[8] Blacks began to add the traditions of Africa to the Baptist and Methodist faiths, and the outcome was Spiritual churches after the Civil War. At this time there was a change in black religious beliefs.

> Much to the dismay of the Catholic Church officials, during this period, local Negroes began to leave the Catholic Church, however, periodically its position of backing off segregation in the 1880's worked against the appeal to Negroes who were more attracted to the rigid segregated Baptist and Methodist churches, where they could organize and shape their separate black congregations. Many of them also associated the Catholic Church with slavery days or with the anti-Negro Irish laborers.[9]

---

[5] John Blassingame, Black New Orleans 1860-1880 (Chicago: University of Chicago Press, 1973), 83.

[6] Ibid., P. 174

[7] John Blassingame, The Slave Community (New York: Oxford University Press, 1972), 69.

[8] Ibid.

[9] Dorothy Rose Eagleson, Some Aspects of the Social Life of the New Orleans Negro in the 1880's, (M. A. Thesis, Tulane University, 1961), 7-9.

The difference of the Catholic Church in North America and South America would produce two distinct religions in the black community in America because the small number of blacks in relation to the white population had an effect on the Catholic Church. The Catholic Church in the south, because of strict segregation, would create the conditions that would bring forth the Spiritual churches in New Orleans. "Latin American slaves became nominal Catholics while largely returning to their African religious beliefs, languages and cultures. Consequently, the Latin Americanization of the slave was no comparison to the Americanization of the bondsman in the south."[10]

The religion of Negroes in New Orleans had a Latin flavor. Specifically slaves from Haiti added their flavor to the religion of Negroes in New Orleans. The Spiritualist churches can be distinguished on the basis of three criteria: the first is the African culture; second, on the religious patterns in Euro-American cultures, and finally on the religious responses on the part of blacks in their minority status in American society.[11]

Spiritualism is recorded as beginning in upstate New York, a decade after the Revolutionary War with the Fox sisters, Leah, Catherine and Margaret Fox. This movement spread to other cities including New Orleans. It was comparable to African religion, because of its spiritual orientation, a belief that the spirit of the

---

[10] John W. Blassingame, The Slave Community, (New York: Oxford University Press, 1972), 70.

[11] Hans Baer, The Black Spiritual Movement: A Religious Response to Racism, (Knoxville, University of Tennessee Press, 1984), 6.

deceased may remain active in the world. The Negro in the south this belief retained from his West African religions.[12]

Religion in black life has developed a unique leader in the black community. The preacher-politician has been and still is a power broker in black politics. W.E.B. Dubois in his Soul of Black Folk described this individual as being a unique person. "The preacher is the most unique personality developed by the Negro on American soil. A leader, a politician, an orator, a boss, an intriguer, an idealist - all these he is and even too, the center of a group of men now twenty, now a thousand members. The combination of a certain deep-seated earnestness of tact with consummate ability gives him preeminence and helps him maintain it.[13]

New Orleans experienced lawlessness during Reconstruction and Redemption. During Reconstruction the rule of the riot was displayed in the 1866 riot in the city. The 1866 riot in the city where the white Democrats murdered white Republicans and Blacks. The period of Redemption saw the leaders of society take up violence as a means to regain political power. The Bourbons resorted to murder and violence to gain control of city's government. By 1896 the rule of the ring, the planters and the merchant politicians, in New Orleans ended. The end of the ring politics in New Orleans signaled the end of black participation in the electoral politics. Both the regulars and the reformers had courted the Negro vote. By the 1890's, hardening of white racial prejudices had come to fruition all over the state. In 1890, the Louisiana Legislature passed its

---

[12] Ibid., P. 19

7

first Jim Crow Law that restricted black passengers to separate seating on railroad cars. In 1894, the state passed a law against miscegenation.[14]

Thus, Louisiana entered the 1900's with the Negro having little political power. The New Orleans blacks protested vigorously against the Jim Crow Laws by challenging segregation in the transportation industry and by protesting public facility segregation laws. Disfranchisement came because of two specific developments; the Constitution of 1898 and the White Primary in 1906. In the gubernatorial election of April, 1896, there had been 130,344 registered Negro voters in Louisiana. In 1900, there were only 5,320 registered Negroes in the state. The 1904 registration list showed 1,342 Negro voters. The institution of the Democratic White primary in 1906 meant virtually the end of Negro voting in Louisiana for many years.[15]

The era of lynching and white supremacy in the city was agitated by the white owned newspapers, the New Orleans Picayune and the Times Democrat, which continuously vilified and ridiculed the Negro. Describing blacks as "niggers, darkies and sambos" the papers courted the prejudice of the white majority.[16]

Africans did not shed all of their religious beliefs and practices when they were introduced to Christianity. These beliefs and practices were transmitted from generation to generation by oral traditions and symbolism. Some African religious ideas were preserved and harmonized with the Christianity of White

---

[13] W. E. B. DuBois, The Soul of Black Folk, (Chicago: A. C. McClung and Co., 1903), 17.
[14] Joy A. Jackson, New Orleans in the Gilded Cage. (Baton Rouge: LSU Press, 1969). 318.
[15] Report of the Secretary of the State of Louisiana, 1906. (Baton Rouge, 1906), 555.
[16] Blassingame, Black New Orleans, 160

Americans, thus producing a unique black form of Christianity. [17] The city of New Orleans set aside Congo Square, a place where slaves could dance. This square was the center of the African dance and rituals in New Orleans.

"There was probably more African survival in the music and dance in Louisiana than in any other areas. Apparently, Louisiana encouraged this for in 1817 the City Council of New Orleans set aside a special place for slaves to dance." [18] The African dances were part of their culture, which contain certain religious connotation.

The turn of the century in 1900 continued a period with little black progress. The years between 1890 and 1910 are regarded as a Nadir period. It was in this period that the blacks in New Orleans were oppressed to a point of revolt. The revolt was in the form of messianic religious prophecy. In 1896, the U.S. Supreme Court handed down its famous ruling in the Plessy vs. Ferguson case establishing the separate accommodation of blacks and whites in transportation. Black suffrage also disappeared in Louisiana after the 1898 Constitutional Convention. By 1900, there were only a few thousand Negro voters remaining. "In his The Negro in America Life and Thought: The Nadir, 1877-1901. . . Rayford W. Logan named the quarter century after Reconstruction, the Nadir for African Americans because of the periods increasing brutality and decreasing prospects for racial harmony and justice."[19] Between 1890 and 1910, southern states passed laws which disenfranchised

---

[17] Timothy E. Fulop and Albert J. Robotean, African American Religion, (New York: Routledge Press, 1977), 299.
[18] Blassingame, Slave Community, p. 36.

9

African Americans and condoned lynching and other forms of racial suppression. The Supreme Court in the case of Plessy vs. Fegerson, upheld the Jim Crow Laws of Louisiana, which the black people of New Orleans fought. This battle had been ongoing during the Nadir from 1898 to 1900. The Council of God had this type of spiritual flavor in its rituals. "Black millennialism during the Nadir period exhibits great variety. . . Cultural Millennialism, Ethiopianism Millennialism and Progressive Millennialism."[20]

The Black religious appeal takes on the millennialism of the Nadir period and from this developed different religious concepts. During the Nadir, many Black Americans differed on how they understood their destiny in different types of millennialism, but they were united in the strong belief that God was in control of history and their future. Bishop Henry M. Turner, of Georgia at the end of the 1800's, a Black Methodist Bishop, presented the rise of black consciousness among blacks most forcefully. The fact that a Methodist Bishop preached that God and Jesus were black was the beginning of Black Theology. The Council of God, a movement of blacks beginning in 1898, also promulgated Black Theology. The influence of Bishop Turner in New Orleans is reflected in the Robert Charles incident of 1900. Robert Charles was a collaborator of Bishop Turner in the late 1890's. Bishop Turner was influential in the south.[21] The Robert Charles incident drew attention from Negroes in New Orleans.

---

[19] Rayford W. Logan, The Negro in American Life and Thought: The Nador. 1877-1901 (New York, Routelege Press), 227.
[20] Fulop and Roboteau, 231.
[21] Ibid.

Robert Charles had a shoot out with the police in 1900 and as a result was a hero to many blacks in the city. The Council of God was also influenced by the of Robert Charles incident. Robert Charles was involved in a shoot out with New Orleans police. He killed thirty-seven people in New Orleans. He was involved in one back to Africa movement in the late 1800's. Marcus Garvey would take up Bishop Turner's "Back to Africa" philosophy in the 1920's. Bishop Turner was a radical bishop in 1900. "The most radical voice in the late nineteenth century was Bishop Henry McNeil Turner of the A.M.E. Church. As an organizer for the Republican Party, Turner helped build a black political base in Georgia. As a theologian, he raised a considerable controversy through his Black Nationalist Liberation Theology that God is a Negro. Turner was the singular voice among the Black clergy that called for reparations for slave labor. He also was a back to African immigrationist".[22]

Bishop Turner asked for reparations for ex-slaves in the 1890's. He asked for a hundred million dollars from the U.S. Congress as payment for the forty billion dollars the United States had received from Negro slavery. He was critical of the Negro for trying to find a home in America.[23]

Bishop Turner contended that the Negro had worked for the white slave master in the United States and had made him rich. According to Turner, because America was one of the great powers of the earth, the Negro who was denied his civil and political rights in the United States, still did not want to separate from America. Bishop Turner called the Negro a fool for wanting to live

---

[22] Ibid.
[23] Ibid.

denied his civil and political rights in the United States, *He* still did not want to

separate from America. Bishop Turner called the Negro a fool for wanting to live

with people who treated him like dogs. The voice of Bishop Turner was heard in

New Orleans. Bishop Turner published the paper, Voice of Mission, and Robert

Charles circulated his ideas of separation in New Orleans. Bishop Turner

preached that the Negro had no rights in this country.

> We are tried in the courts, but the judge and jury are white and
> justice is unknown, if the suit is against a white man or woman.
> Jails are broken into; we are taken out and burned, shot, hanged,
> disjointed and murdered in every way. Our civil rights are taken
> from us by force; our political rights are a farce.[24]

Bishop Turner had a follower in New Orleans that would gain a reputation

for courage. Robert Charles was an activist that promulgated the ideas of Bishop

Turner in New Orleans until his death in 1900. Robert Charles was a

sharecropper from southern Mississippi who moved to New Orleans. He worked

among Negroes in New Orleans doing odd jobs. Martin Berhman was the Mayor

of New Orleans during the time of Robert Charles and the riot he caused. Robert

Charles felt very deeply about the situation of Negroes in the United States.[25]

The Robert Charles incident began while he was visiting a girlfriend and

was attacked by New Orleans' police officers. He carried a gun and when fired

upon by a police officer, he returned fire. The incident excited a riot in the

colored section of town near Saratoga Street. Charles was finally killed after a

crowd of white men gathered to destroy him. He was a determined man. He had

---

[24] John H. Bracey, Jr., <u>Black Nationlism</u>, 173.

[25] Ibid.

vowed that the police would never take him alive to be lynched. Robert Charles shot 27 whites before being killed.[26]

The Robert Charles incident was a prelude to the Council of God incident of 1907. "Counting the Death of Captain Charles now left seven dead (four of whom were police officers), eight seriously wounded (three of whom were police officers, twelve slightly wounded who were not identified by name or occupation. Robert Charles had shot twenty-seven white people since Monday night."[27]

A white mob gathered after the incident on Saratoga Street had ended and killed several innocent blacks. The members of the mob were all acquitted of murder charges. The man who had avenged Charles by killing the informer who had told police where Charles was hiding was given life in prison. The family that had hidden Charles was held in the parish prison for a year.[28]

The incident of Robert Charles produced a legend in the black community. The police of New Orleans had gained the reputation of treating blacks without regard to the law. The brutality of New Orleans police was again tried in 1907 with the Council of God incident.

William Ivy Hair wrote the book Carnival of Fury, Robert Charles and the New Orleans Race Riot of 1900. This book was reviewed by the Journal of American History. In their review they describe the impact of Charles Oddessey as follows:

> One July week of 1900 an obscure Black laborer named Robert Charles drew national headlines when he shot twenty-seven whites including seven policemen in a series of encounters with the New

---

[26] Ibid.
[27] Ibid. 200.
[28] Ibid.

13

Orleans police. Charles became an instant hero among some Blacks, but to most people he was a mysterious and sinister figure who had promoted a Back to Africa movement. Few knew anything about his early life.

This biography of Charles follows him from childhood in a Mississippi sharecropper's cabin to his violent death on New Orleans Saratoga Street. With few clues available William Ivy Hair has forced together the story of a man whose life spanned the thirty-four years from emancipation to 1900. Charles tried to achieve dignity and self-respect in a time when people of his race could not exhibit such characteristics without fear of reprisal.

Carnival of Fury is not a traditional biography, for Charles was not the sort of person to leave behind extensive written records. It is instead a skillful penetrating exploration of the world of Robert Charles, the communities in which he lived, and the daily lives of dozens of people, white and black, who were involved in his Oddessey.[29]

HISTORY OF THE COUNCIL OF GOD

The mother of the Council of God Church in New Orleans was a church called Christ's Church which began in the early 1890's. It was also known as Christ Hebrew Church and the Christian Jewish Church. Out of this organization sprang the Council of God Church around 1903. Christ Church was the creation of Albert Leon Antoine, a Baptist minister who established the church on Carrollton Avenue. Christ Church was established in the early 1890's.[30]

Antoine moved his operation to Congo Square in the Negro Section of New Orleans after his first church was demolished. Congo Square is located near Louis Armstrong Park. The church was demolished because the railroad was routed through that area. Congo Square had been the gathering place of Negroes since slavery times. There were festivals there each year where

---

[29] Hair, Carnival of Fear Review.

to as the Ring Shout, similar to the Israelites' "Battle of Jericho"[31]. The Battle of Jericho, where blacks used this African dance as a ritual to accomplish certain feats.

The names of Antoine's church were many. This identification with the Ancient Hebrews in the Bible was not unusual for African religious groups. The Hebrew Nation had sojourned in Egypt, which was an ancient African civilization; some of the rituals of the Israelites became assimilated all over Africa and had become part of some African traditional religions. Antoine established a church, which was indiscriminately, called Christ Hebrew Church, the Christian Jewish Church and Christ's Council, but was listed under the Baptist sect as Christ Church. Out of this Hebrew Baptist congregation around 1903, sprung the Council of God.[32]

Antoine spread his teachings to many quarters. If one is to understand the black community's infatuation with religious leaders, they must understand that in Africa, leaders are heads of the religious orders and secular governing leaders. Priest/King is seen in African institutions in contrast to warrior/King in the European culture of Europe.[33]

Edward Honore who was one of the influential figures in the Council of God AND was described by a New Orleans newspaper as having an inferiority complex. "One of the earliest officials of the Council of God must have been a disgruntled minor house servant who felt inferiority keenly. The position of head

---

[31] Sterling Stacker, Slave Culture. (New York: Oxford University Press, 1987), 84-85.
[32] W.P.A. Dillion. 4.
[33] Ibid.

butler seemed to have been an enviable rank, higher than a prophet or an apostle, and just one cut below that of high priest. The second ranking title in order was chief butler. So far, above the average member that had lessor aides were biblical characters, direct descendants of those whose name they had the souls of patriarchs of old, having been transmigrated into their bodies. Old men were elected for missionaries."[34]

The Council of God prophets were purported to be divine healers. This attracted blacks because some of the powers attributed to the position of priest in African religions were those of medicine men. Naturally, blacks were familiar with the combined role of the secular and religious. The Council of God gained converts to their church by way of healing the sick. The healing acts of the prophets were believed to reflect the healings of Jesus enumerated in the New Testament who said that thousands who followed him would have even greater power. The Catholic Church recognized miracles and healing power and they regarded those with this ability to heal as saints. The Council of God mixed some of the teachings of Christianity with some of the tenants of Hinduism and Buddhism.[35]

The Council of God recognized as God the spirit that dwelled within man. Heaven and hell were not places in the hereafter. According to their views Heaven was occupied by white men and consisted of earthly pleasure, wealth and power. Hell was inhabited by the Negro and was comprised of the world's misery, poverty, labor and slavery. In time, by the accumulation of money and

---

[34] Ibid. 7.

16

Heaven was occupied by white men and consisted of earthly pleasure, wealth and power. Hell was inhabited by the Negro and was comprised of the world's misery, poverty, labor and slavery. In time, by the accumulation of money and influence, blacks would be able to overthrow the white race and be in Heaven themselves. The church explained that the Negro should not be under the same God as the white man. He should have a God of his own and not having one, the Reverend Antoine thought it behooved man to create one of their own. These and other ideas of the church would later appear in the Marcus Garvey Movement in the 1920's.[36]

According to Antoine the attitude toward the Negro was inspired by the fact that black men did not pray to him, but to the God who wrote the Ten Commandments. The Negro was the true Israelite, the real Jew in whom all promises were fulfilled. Circumcision was one of the basic practices of the church. Antoine claimed that Christ had done this so his followers should also do it. The prophet taught that the Negro birthright had been taken from him by persons professing to be Jews, who bought the name Jew from the Pope of Rome at a time when he ruled the world. The black man labored under the curse of slavery because he respected and killed Christ.[37]

In Antoine's view the Pope of Rome came into being after the death of Jesus. The true Jews are not what today are looked upon as Israel because these people have the religion of tradition but not the culture of Egypt, which is an African creation. Many of Antoine's teachings have their roots in African

---

[36] Ibid. 5.

religions beginning with the teachings of the Grand Temple Secret Society of Ancient Egypt. The Ten Commandments were extracted out of the book known as the Book of the Dead by Western Scholars. The cornerstone of ancient Egyptian religious teaching was "know thy self".[38]

The Council of God had its commandments: First, honor they father and thy mother and thy God; Second, thou shall obey the prophets and teach their preaching's; Third, the last shall be first and the first shall be last, that the black man was his own God and his children and his own; Fourth, multiply with disciples of the Council of God; Fifth and Sixth dealt with free love and equality among members.[39]

The Council of God conducted feasts on different days of the week. The days of the week were all feast days. The calendar was as follows:

> First Day, Feast of Canaanites.
> Second Day, Feast of Hittites.
> Third Day, Feast of Ammonites.
> Fourth Day, Feast of Perizzites.
> Fifth Day, Feast of Hevites.
> Sixth Day, Feast of Jebasites.
> Seventh Day, Feast of Israelites.[40]

The Council of God had burial and marriage ceremonies. These rituals reflected African origins. They looked upon the black woman as a queen. This gave the members self-esteem, because it was social redemption from the days

---

[37] Ibid. 5
[38] Ibid.
[39] Ibid.
[40] Ibid. 8.

of slavery. During slavery, the black man did not protect black women from the

advances of white slave masters.[41]

THE CONFRONTATION

"A dream or vision, which awakened Robert J. Cambias from sleep Friday evening shortly before nightfall, was vividly recalled last night by his bereaved parents. The gallant young officer had related the strange dream to them before he went to answer roll call and begin on his last night of watch.   Such a seemingly supernatural warning of harm from Negroes as the young officer had, would have been sufficient to have made most men especially careful to keep out of possible collisions with any set of blacks. Cambias disregarded the warning and even laughed at it. He was to become the victim of fanatical Negroes. He was killed trying to arrest Negroes at the Council of God meeting."[42]

There are two important interpretations of what happened on October 18,

1907 in New Orleans. The Council of God members stated that all the police

officers came together and they attempted to arrest all that was there and a shot

rang out after the lights were turned off. Robert Cambias grabbed one of the

men and pulled the man with him as he left. Two men are said to have grabbed

him, he drew his revolver and then he was killed with a knife. This happened on

a night when the Council of God was celebrating a wedding of two of its

members. A meeting was held at Chief Butler's house in 1809 on New Orleans

Street, which stood near a vacant lot. They were celebrating a feast called the

Queen's Crowning.[43]

The children in the neighborhood threw stones, bricks and mud at the

house where the Council of God was meeting. Three missiles were believed to

have been thrown from across the street where some young white boys were

playing. A brick landed on the roof and a lump of dry mud fell in the midst of the

---

[41] Ibid.
[42] Daily Picayune (New Orleans), October 21, 1907. p. 1

meeting. The black men were angered. It was written in their commandments that anyone not of their faith who disturbed them should die.[44]

This appeared to be the account made up by people who saw the church as causing racial conflict. There never was any evidence produced that they, the church, had such a commandment. The members were said to exclaim they had their own laws and their own God; they did not call the police for help. They enforced their commandments themselves.[45]

After coming out of the Council of God meeting, it was alleged by others that Honore and Pierre, both members of the Council of God, came upon and attacked a young man named John Sherman. Sherman was cut but not seriously injured. If that many men with razors and knives attacked a young officer as the newspaper described, then surely Sherman would have been seriously injured. Sherman was alleged to have gone and returned with Officer Cambias. Cambias attempted to arrest the alleged assailant. Cambias is quoted as saying, "I don't care how bad they are, I am going to arrest the one that cut you or they'll kill me."[46] Cambias got into a brawl with Honore, Lattimore Boyd and Jack Pierre and was killed. Cambias' jugular vein and several arteries were severed. The next event that is alleged to have occurred was that the men went inside the house cursing and bragging that they killed a policeman. It is not

---

[43] Ibid.
[44] W.P.A. Dillon. 14
[45] Ibid.
[46] Ibid. 15.

possible that during this period of 1907 any Negroes would kill a policeman and walk off thinking that nothing would become of it.[47]

According to the local press, "Fifteen minutes later after word had been received at the 5th Precinct Station on Elysian Fields Avenue, Sergeant Joseph Wheatley and Corporal William Peterson, both hardly more than boys, reached the scene to look for Cambias and stumbled over his body."[48]

There were reports saying that these men were merely boys. What happened next seemed to be a police account of what happened that night. Sam Davis, (a member of the Council of God) who had often claimed that no policeman would arrest him, shouted, "We'll kill forty policemen before we move an inch." [49] "Wheatley seized him and started toward the door." Davis, a giant like Negro, grappled with the officer and turmoil reigned as the lights went out and the blacks closed in on the plucky young Sergeant. A shot rang out and found a mark in Wheatley's chest. Corporal Peterson armed with a double-barreled shotgun, reached to assist his companion with one arm as he opened fire on the Negroes with the other. Someone slumped under a load of buckshot. It was Chief Butler Edward Honore.[50]

When two other officers arrived, they were overwhelmed and injured. Injured were Corporal James E. Dunn and Patrolman Ernest Wench. Wench

---

[47] Ibid.
[48] Daily Picayune. (New Orleans), October 31, 1907. p. 4.
[49] W.P.A. Dillon, p. 16.
[50] Ibid.

was cut and shot. There was gunfire from the church as the officers retreated around the corner.[51]

When the news of the riot spread, detectives were rushed to assist the young officers and reinforcements under the leadership of Police Secretary George Vindaworst arrived at the scene. Captain Boyle and Gaps took out a patrol wagon full of men armed with shotguns. Volleys of bullets erupted from the shanty to welcome each new contingent of policemen that ventured near the house.[52]

The revolt of the Council of God caught the policemen unprepared to deal with an armed band of Negroes. While the battle raged, some Negroes escaped through a rear window. There were women and children in the house. The incident attracted crowds from nearby streets. The crowd made the policemen's job more complicated. The crowds included were white men bent on lynching the two Negroes. It was decided by these whites to burn the Negroes out. Cries went up to fire the house and smoke out the Negro devils. A hole was burned in the fence between the neighboring hut that was fired and the Negro stronghold. Corporal Peterson, with a double-barreled shotgun, watched for any movement from within the meeting place. A man appeared in the doorway and a blast from Peterson's gun felled him. Then at the cry of "rush them", the officers stormed the place. The blacks surrendered and the first prisoner was taken. Thomas Manson was the first to be arrested. One by one, the others were dragged from

---

[51] Ibid.
[52] Ibid. 17.

22

the place, some were found in the nearby house.[53] This riot shook New Orleans in 1907. After the capture of the Council of God, the newspapers portrayed them as ignorant and stupid Negroes. They were portrayed as coming from the lower ranks of New Orleans' black community. Blacks who wanted to keep in the good graces of the white society also attacked them in the local newspaper. This set the prelude to the trial.[54]

The fact that the leaders of the Council of God were selected to pay for the killing of the policemen is the method of terminating any movement. Killing the leaders of any mass movement perpetrated the death of any movement that defied the status quo in the south, and the tyranny over black people in the south during this era. The media was foremost in the conviction of someone for the death of white policemen. The trial would be preceded by an avalanche of criticism and accusations in the white owned newspaper in New Orleans.

Chapter II

The Newspapers before the Trial

The newspapers in New Orleans condemned the Council of God before the actual trial. The Daily Picayune tried and convicted the defendants Honore

---

[53] Ibid. 28.

and Pierre in its columns. This chapter will attempt to establish that the Daily Picayune and Time Democrat were the jury before the trial began. The main point of this paper is that Honore and Pierre were not guilty of murder, and Edward Honore could be found to have acted in self-defense. This paper also will attempt to prove that Jack Pierre was innocent of the charge of murder. The newspapers had so influenced the white citizens of New Orleans that it was impossible for the two defendants, Honore and Pierre, to have received justice in the courts. The two daily newspapers, The Daily Picayune and Times Democrat acted as judge and jury in the case. The make-up of the jury was the traditional all white jury. This paper will show that the newspapers of New Orleans acted out of prejudice against blacks in their reporting of this incident. The newspapers depicted blacks as having no humanity, but were brutal beasts who murdered a policeman acting in the line of duty. The description of Honore was a prejudiced account of him being a monster. "Honore, the great black Negro, who has a head shaped like an ape, seems imbedded with the strange religion followed by what he and other blacks call the Council of God, and also argue that he and his brethren and sisters in the sect are much abused. His wounds were not serious, and there is likelihood that he will be out of the hospital in a short while and made to stand trial for the murder of policeman Cambias and the wounding of the other blue coat."[55]

The Times Democrat depicted the Council of God as being a frantic group of debased Negroes. The membership of the Council of God was accused of

---

[54] Ibid.

being of the lowest ring of Negroes that emerged from the deepest pit of black

ignorance.   The beliefs of the group were described as being strange and

demonic.

> Negroes - Revile Deity, would enslave whites; Dangerous Fanaticism of
> Council of God. Cult responsible for murder of one officer and the
> wounding of others, seek to embitter ignorant blacks against the white
> race - Rejoice when told that murder has been committed; Strange beliefs
> of Honore's followers. A terrible religion born of an almost bottomless
> ignorance, such as is only possible with the lowest order of blacks which
> has been fanned into a fanatic frenzy by leaders who themselves hardly
> understood the coherent tenets of their strange faith, and which has for its
> supreme purpose the ultimate annihilation or subjugation of the whites.[56]

The Times Democrat described the interrogation of the men involved in

the death of the policeman. The contradictory accounts were used as evidence

of the guilt of both Honore and Jack Pierre.

> Five men implicated. The evidence connecting these men with the crime
> and subsequent shooting given to the police at the Fifth Precinct Station is
> conflicting. Some of the Negroes when sweated declared that Boyd was
> the man who knelt upon the prostrate form of the unfortunate young
> patrolman and held him while Honore plunged his murderous dirk into his
> neck. Others declare that Sam Davis was the man who held Cambias,
> and that Pierre supplemented Honore's work by mutilating Cambias'
> helpless body with a razor.[57]

The newspaper never mentioned the fact that the officer that was killed

tried to kill Honore, but his gun did not fire. The conflicting stories were elicited

from the members of the Council of God without a lawyer to defend them.

> Jacques Pierre and Robert Slaughter also prominent figures in the fight,
> according to those who testified before the police yesterday and their work
> were invaluable in rousing the members of God's Council to a frenzy to
> attack the officers. The foundation upon which the God's Council was
> erected was one of murder; that the sole goal inspired to be the

---

[55] Daily Picayune, (New Orleans) October 20, 1907, P. 7.
[56] Times Democrat, (New Orleans) October 20, 1907, P. 5.
[57] Ibid.

extermination and the subsequent subjugation of whites. That the society acknowledges no God: that its beliefs were as fanatical as were the ancient mysteries of voodoo times: those branches of the organization were scattered throughout other southern cities.[58]

What frightened the whites of New Orleans was that they did not know the actual number of Negroes who were a part of this movement. The newspaper also misrepresented the Council of God not believing in God. The real fear of whites in New Orleans was that blacks did not believe the tenets of religion taught by most black Baptist and Methodist churches. The black main line churches did not teach blacks to look for a different God from the one whites believed. The creation of African religions among blacks in the U.S.A. had left blacks with only the Bible as the book that contained divine knowledge. God to the black Baptist and Methodist was the same God that the Gentile White Europeans had taught them to worship. The author agrees with Marx that religion was the opium of the people. The use of a black clergyman to refute the ideas of Council of God was the usual use of black preachers to apologize for blacks who stepped out of line with the traditional response of Negroes.

> Colored Baptists denounced the Council of God audits teaching. The colored Baptist ministers met yesterday and adopted the following. Resolved by the Baptist ministers conference of New Orleans that the recent developments that have come to light in the past few days have revealed to us the fact that a dangerous and pernicious doctrine under the guise of religion has been inculcated on the minds of a certain band of ignorant colored people, styling themselves, the Council of God, which has caused them to be guilty of one of the most revolting crimes that has ever occurred in our city.[59]

---

[58] Ibid.
[59] Daily Picayune (New Orleans) October 25, 1907, P. 11

The leaders of the Council of God did not forget about the murder of Negroes after the police had killed Robert Charles in 1900. The police searched the houses of the leaders of the Council of God for incriminating evidence but only found a copy of the New Orleans telegram dated July 28, 1900, which gave a complete account of the killing of the Negro desperado Robert Charles by the police.[60]

The New Orleans newspapers were convinced that the leaders of the Council were guilty of murder. The Council of God was described as a conspiring group of Negroes by the newspapers. The daughter of Honore was quoted as saying that her father told her he had killed the policeman. The newspaper described the evidence against the leaders of the Council of God as being irrefutable. The paper said that only a fickle minded jury would find them innocent.[61]

The Daily Picayune assumed the guilt of Honore and Pierre as it reported on the prospect of their being hanged.

> Council of God cure gives Boyd lockjaw the Negro who held officer Cambias, during brutal murder may cheat the gallows. . . . However the Negro would not allow the bandages and ointment of the devil doctor. The name applied to the white physician, to remain on his foot. . . . The preliminary examination of the Negroes implicated in the murder of patrolman Cambias will occur today. Boyd was one of the men who is said to have held Cambias while Edward Honore cut his throat. District Attorney Porter Parker inquired of the condition of the Negro yesterday afternoon, and was keenly disappointed. However the stress will be relentlessly prosecuted and even if death from lockjaw cheats the gallows,

---

[60] Dillion, W.P.A., Northwestern State University Watson Library, Cammie G. Henry Research Center, P. 20.

[61] Ibid., October 6, 1907. P. 1.

27

the evidence against Honore and Jack Pierre makes it almost certain that they will be prey for the grim instrument.[62]

The newspapers contained allegations of murder when the trial began. They stated that the testimony of the Negro followers of Honore and Jack Pierre would convict them of murder. They used statements about hanging Negroes before a jury was called.

> The coils of the hangman's noose draw tighter around the black throats of Edward Honore and Jack Pierre, Apostle Paul. When the two black families of the Council of God were brought before the bar of the second city criminal court yesterday to answer for the brutal murder of patrolman Robert J. Cambias, whose throat was slashed while he was attempting to place one of the blacks under arrest.[63]

The newspapers made it nearly impossible for Honore and Pierre to get a fair trial. The newspapers commented on the hanging of the two before a trial was in progress.

The actual indictment by the court was reported in the Daily Picayune in October. The proceeding as described by the newspaper assumed that the defendants were guilty. They still continued to describe the Council of God as a group of religious fanatics.

> The Grand Jury met yesterday and took up the Council of God Case. After hearing a number of witnesses they found a true bill against Edward Honore and Jacques Pierre for the murder of the late patrolman Cambias, and then adjourned until the first Thursday in December next, having nothing before them. They wanted to call, but Judge Chretien suggested that they adjourn to some fixed date as they were always subject to call. After consulting among themselves they decided upon December 5th. When they will hold their session in Judge Baker's court, that section meeting on the first Monday in December next.[64]

---

[62] Ibid., November 7, 1907, P.1.

[63] Ibid., P. 5.

[64] Ibid.

The trial of Edward Honore was described by the Daily Picayune as being rail roaded through the court. The proceedings began on a morning and concluded by afternoon. The defense had no witnesses to call. The council that represented Honore had no time to prepare a defense. The lawyer representing Honore did not request more time to prepare his defense. However, the defense did offer the suggestion that Honore acted in self defense as one of the main witnesses noted Cambias did snap his gun in Honore's face before he was killed. The defense council did not raise the point that Cambias was acting without a warrant when he came to Honore's house.

> Council of God Prophet tried for police murder. Edward Honore first of the fanatics to face jury for awful crime, admits grappling with Cambias, but charges other Negroes with stabbing. Jury locked up for the night. The fate of Edward Honore, known as the Prophet and leader of the sect of religious fanatics called the Council of God is in the hands of a jury. The case was called yesterday morning at 10 o'clock before Judge Chretien in section b of the Criminal District Court. Little time was consumed in the selection of a jury today. The Negroes was very nervous when the noon hour rolled by the jury box was almost filled, and at 10 o'clock the panel was complete. Judge Chretien ordered a recess. When court convened the state railroad its case and at 5 o'clock District Attorney Porter Parker closed.[65]

The lawyer that represented Honore had but one defense and that was self-defense. "Judge Henry D. Hollander, who represented the prisoner, announced that he had but one witness to place on the stand and that his argument would be brief. Judge Hollander argued that the Negro acted in self defense."[66]

The fact that Honore was poor apparently worked to his disadvantage.

---

[65] Ibid., P. 13
[66] Ibid.

29

Honore a poor man could not afford to engage counsel, and it proved a difficult matter for him to obtain the necessary legal talent to offer a defense for him. Pleading informal paupers before the court, Judge Henry D. Hollander was assigned as his counsel, and he though reluctant accepted the trust, with his usual diligence he did everything in his power to defend his client. B.B. Howard at his request became associate counsel and a young attorney named Viosed was the third of the attorneys who appeared yesterday morning at the bar in behalf of Honore.[67]

The newspapers mentioned nothing about the fact that several of the witnesses testified that officer Cambias snapped his gun in the defendant Edward Honore's face before he was grabbed. Honore admitted that he cut the officer, but denied it was he who fatally stabbed the officer.

> Edward Honore first of the Fanatics to face Jury for awful crime, admits grappling with Cambias, but charge other Negroes with stabbing. Jury locked up for the night. The fate of Edward Honore, known as the Prophet and leader of the sect of religious fanatics called the Council of God, is in the hands of the jury. The case was called yesterday morning at 10 o'clock before Judge Chretien.[68]

The Daily Picayune described the proceedings without presenting the facts of what happened that night. Henry Boyd the state's star witness testified that the officer snapped his gun at Honore before the scuffle. The attorneys for Edward Honore called no witnesses to defend him. At the trial Honore admitted he cut the officer, but contended that he did not kill him. Pierre claimed he never touched the officer. A witness, Henry Boyd, admitted he never saw Pierre hold or cut Cambias.[69]

> Honore testified-but as he raised his hand Pierre plunged the dirk into the officer's neck. He said that the officer fell just outside the gate. The

---

[67] Ibid.

[68] Ibid.

[69] Ibid.

witness was subjected to a rigid cross-examination by Mr. Parker and Mr. Mooney. He denied that he had admitted that he had a razor in his hand. He also denied having wiped the blood from the dirk on the bed. He said if he had known before hand that there would be trouble he would not have gone into the yard. Honore said that he had been shot by the police, and had not entirely recovered from the wound. Judge Hollander argued that the Negro acted in self-defense. Judge Hollander rested his entire case on Honore's testimony.[70]

In the trial Honore admitted that he cut Cambias. He contended that he had his back turned when the incident occurred. Jack Pierre asked for a severance of his case from Honore's. There were two trials but one grand jury action. Henry Boyd, a member of the Council of God, was the prosecution's star witness. He stated in his testimony that the officer pulled his revolver on Honore.

> The only eyewitness seated in the closet near the gate was Henry Boyd, who was really the only eyewitness to the struggle. He saw a dagger in the hands of Honore and a razor in the hands of John Pierre and these two with a third Negro, since dead attacked Cambias, who drew his revolver. Cambias, however, was unable to use it, one Negro seizing him by both arms, while the other two cut him.[71]

Henry Boyd in his testimony as recorded by the state; maintained he never saw the killing. He only assumed they cut the officer. George Gaspar, another witness, was only aware that the officer was backed up in a corner. Jack Pierre called for a separate trial. The conduct of the trial of Pierre was more difficult for the prosecution. Jack Pierre's trial was on February 12, 1908.

> When Judge Chretien opened court promptly at 10:30 o'clock yesterday morning he ordered Honore to be called and then sent for the jury. He had been informed that the jurors wanted the evidence of some of the witnesses read over to them. It seems as though there was some misunderstanding about one point in the testimony of Boyd, and this they wanted to settle. When the jury returned they asked that the testimony of Henry Boyd be read. They also heard the testimony of Dave Major, a

---

[70] Ibid.
[71] Ibid.

31

witness for the state . . . . He handed the fateful document to Judge Chretein, who glanced at it, and returning it to the minute clerk asked the foreman to sign the verdict. The foreman complied, and the minute clerk then read the words guilty as charged. Honore received the fiat in silence, and without any outward sign of perturbation.[72]

The trial of Jack Pierre, as reported by the newspaper, was longer than Honore's trial. In Pierre's trial the first witness was Dr. Joseph O'Hara.

> William H. Luzenberg represented Pierre and District Attorney Parker and his Assistant Henry Mooney conducted the case on behalf of the State. Considerable time was taken up in the selection of a jury, and it was 4 o'clock in the afternoon when the hearing opened. Dr. Joseph O'Hara was the first witness called, his testimony being precisely the same as that given at the trial of Honore, which was that Cambias had come to his death by two incised wounds of the left side of the neck, severing the jugular vein and carotid artery.[73]

The newspaper portrayed Henry Boyd as being sharp of mind in his testimony against the two defendants. "He had admitted that he was Father Abraham of the Bible. He also stated that once he was a Greek. However, at the present time was a nigger, suh."[74]

The Daily Picayune's account of the trial of Jack Pierre credited Henry Boyd with being the star witness for the prosecution.

> Pierre on trial now for Cambias' murder. Henry Boyd the Father Abraham, again star witness. Two thousand years old and knows his Bible. This is the second of The Council of God cases to be tried in this section. Jack Pierre was one of the three Negroes who attacked Robert J. Cambias, late patrolman of the Fifth Precinct after he entered the yard of the premises sublet to the sect known as the Council of God, of which the so-called prophet was Edward Honore, tried last month and convicted. Pierre who was jointly charged with Honore with the murder of the officer asked for a severance, which was granted, and the case was fixed for yesterday.[75]

---

[72] Ibid., February 1, 1908. P. 5.

[73] Ibid., February 12, 1908. P. 5.

[74] Ibid.

[75] Ibid.

The newspaper account was very prejudiced against Honore and Pierre. The newspaper account of the testimony of Ernest Bertonnier, and Dave Majors will be compared with the actual testimony of these witnesses at the Grand Jury hearing. The newspaper's account of the testimony of Ernest Bertonnier was that he was seated on the doorstep of the house not very far away, when Officer Cambias was cut. He saw the motions of three Negroes as they fell upon and sliced Cambias. He was cursing the Negroes when they cut him. The boy, John Sherman, was running away when he heard Cambias curse the Negroes. Bertonnier testified that he had warned Cambias to be careful and not enter the place. He said that he sat near the corner and saw Cambias march through the gate.[76]

The testimony of Dave Majors another member of the Council of God was taken. He appeared to give an account that would clear himself. He never mentioned Jack Pierre in his testimony as doing anything to the officer. Majors said, however, that Honore had come in the room with his dagger all bloody.

According to Majors:

Well, the police came and stood in the door, and he asked who cut that boy. There were some of the members sitting on a bench, and I saw them grab the officer by the neck and shove him out the door. One of the elders said that they were just putting him on the street. Then Honore come in, and his dagger was all bloody. The elder asked him what had he done and Honore said: I cut his neck. The Elder told Honore, that he had done his work well, and that there would be others to get their necks cut before long.[77]

---

[76] Ibid., P. 13.
[77] Ibid.

This testimony contradicted that of earlier witnesses in that Cambias was first confronted with Honore. The testimony of Sherman stated that the officer asked who had cut the boy and for him to point out the culprit. Officer Cambias was acting without a warrant and only on the words of Sherman.[78]

The following is the testimony of Ernest Bertonnier, a New Orleans policeman and a witness for the state, as he was sworn for the prosecution. He was examined by District Attorney Parker.

> Q. What occurred that evening as far as you saw it.
> A. Well, I was there, I went with him back there, I heard some arrest was to be made back there, took the boy and we went back there and he went inside and said to me stay back don't come with me in the yard, he said to me sit on the steps. I was sitting down there and he went inside and he came out with the prisoner; this man right here.
> Q. What is his Name?
> A. Honore.[79]

The facts are conflicting; some of the witnesses say Honore was holding the officer and some say that Pierre was holding him. Parker continued the questioning.

> Q. Honore.
> A. Honore, when he was coming out with the man on the banquette this man here, this fellow here.
> Q. Jack Pierre.
> A. Jack Pierre and some other man, I don't know who he was, they grabbed the policeman from the back and they over powered him, and threw him down. I stayed there a while; I stayed there a half hour afterwards.
> Q. Did you see what they were doing to him when they threw him down?
> A. No, sir, only I saw this man was making motions with his arm working it like that.

---

[78] Ibid.

[79] State of Louisiana vs. Edward Honore Criminal District Court, Parish of Orleans, New Orleans, Louisiana. P. 4.

Q.	You mean this man Jack Pierre.
A.	Yes sir.
Q.	Did you see what Honore was doing?
A.	No sir, I couldn't see they were holding him."[80]
Q.	Never mind what he said to you. Did you see any darkies come out through that gate afterwards?
A.	No sir, no one at all no one at all.
Q.	You stayed out there a half hour and the officer never got up from where you saw him?
A.	No sir.
	Question from Jack Pierre. You say you saw me out there?
A.	Yes, I did.
Q.	Well, I was not out there at all. Questioning by the Judge: Never mind contradicting him, you have got to stand by his answer, you may disapprove it but you can't deny it. By Mr. Honore - when you took me under arrest, I surrendered to him, I went out with him, and I went out with him. By the Judge that is a statement that is not asking any questions. This is where a good lawyer could have helped Honore and Pierre's case if they had one. This witness contradicted the testimony of Mr. Henry Boyd. Boyd testified that Honore didn't hold the man or officer, but Pierre and T. Boyd did.

The next witness in the court records was Henry Boyd, sworn for

the prosecution. The direct examination was by Parker.

Q.	You were a member of this Council of God were you not?
A.	Yes sir.
Q.	You were known as Father Abraham?
A.	Yes sir.
Q.	You were there the night that this police officer was killed weren't you?
A.	Yes sir, I was.
Q.	Where were you at the time that the officer came to the gate?
A.	At the time the office came to the gate, I was in the water closet.
Q.	The water closet is near the gate isn't it?
A.	Yes, near the gate about from here to the back of that chair there, I suppose.
Q.	After the officer came in the gate what did he do? Did you see anybody lay hands on him? What occurred?

---

[80] Ibid.

A.   When the officer came into the gate, Old Honore came to the gate, came inside and said we are not doing anything to cause trouble and they clinched.[81]

The next series of questions confirm the accusations of the prosecutor.

Q.   Who clinched?
A.   They clinched the officer.
Q.   Then what did they do?
A.   Well the last I saw of them they were last backing him out the gate and when I seen him fall.
Q.   Who the officer?
A.   The officer fell on the ground. I saw Honore on top of him with the knife cutting his throat.[82]
Q.   What was Pierre doing? Did he have hold of him?
A.   Pierre was holding him and Mr. Boyd both.
Q.   The one you call Latimore Boyd, a member of the Council of God, is he the man who is dead now?
A.   Yes sir.
Q.   Did you see the officer draw his pistol in the yard?
A.   I did.
Q.   What became of the pistol in the yard? Did you see it?
A.   Honore had taken the pistol out of his hand when he cut his throat.
Q.   When he was down?
A.   Yes sir.
Q.   It was out in the yard that he drew his pistol?
A.   Out in the yard. He was backed up in the corner by the gate, he was backed up in the corner there and they took hold of him and they took him out and he done took his pistol out in the street.
Q.   When he drew his pistol, did you see anybody take his arms?
A.   Yes sir, Boyd grabbed his arms.
Q.   That stopped him from shooting didn't it?
A.   I suppose.
Q.   You saw them throw him down?
A.   Yes sir, I never went, I just come out of the privy door and I never went a distance of any more from here to this door.[83]
      Now Pierre asks a question of Henry Boyd.
      Question by Pierre.
Q.   Father Abraham, you say you saw me out there?

[81] Ibid., P. 6.
[82] State of Louisiana vs. Honore, Section B, Criminal District Court of Orleans 1908. P.7.
[83] Ibid.

36

A.	I saw you and Ferdinand Boyd both.
Q.	You saw Ferdinand Boyd and Honore and me?
A.	Yes sir.
Q.	You didn't see me there because when I went out there it was Boyd out there and Apostle Paul and Honore.
	By the court. I asked you if you want to ask him any questions.
A.	I only saw you and Boyd and Honore.
Q.	You saw that I had a razor in my hand.
A.	Yes sir.
Q.	I didn't have no razor in my hand; I had a piece of horsehair.[84]

This ended Henry Boyd's testimony. The next witness called by the state

was Joseph Gasper.

Q.	You were present on the night that this trouble occurred on the 18th of October weren't you?
A.	I just come in.
Q.	Were you in the yard when the officer came in?
A.	Yes sir, I was right by the steps.
Q.	By the steps?
A.	Yes sir.
Q.	By the steps?
A.	The steps right under the house.
Q.	What room, where the meeting was held?
A.	Yes sir.
Q.	When the officer comes in there did you see Honore, Jack Pierre and Boyd?
A.	I seen Boyd, Apostle Paul and Ed.
Q.	Honore?
A.	Yes sir.
Q.	Apostle Paul you mean Latimore?
A.	Yes sir.
Q.	He is the man that is dead?
A.	Yes sir.
Q.	Did you see Jack Pierre?
A.	Yes sir, I seen him, I seen Jack Pierre, after he come back in the room when the policeman was cut.[85]
Q.	When the policeman came in the yard did you see any of them do anything to him?

---

[84] Ibid., P. 9.
[85] Ibid., P. 10.

A.	The policeman come there an told him, he says, I come here to arrest you, and Apostle Paul got up and then Honore got him and brought him outside.
Q.	Where was Jack Pierre?
A.	Jack Pierre was in the yard.
Q.	Did you see him do anything to the officer?
A.	I didn't see him do anything to the officer no sir, not at that time.
Q.	Who did you say you saw take the officer out in the yard.
A.	Apostle Paul and Ed Honore.
Q.	You didn't see what occurred out on the sidewalk, outside the gate, did you see when they had the officer out there?
A.	They brought him out there and threw him down; I saw when they threw him down from inside out to the gate.
Q.	Could you see what they were doing to him out there?
A.	No sir.
Q.	After the officer was thrown down, where did you go?
A.	I was still remaining at that door, in the room door.
Q.	The door of his room?
A.	Yes sir.
Q.	Did he have anything in his hand?
A.	He had a revolver in his hand.
Q.	Did you see Jack Pierre come back in there?
A.	Jack Pierre came back in there.
Q.	Did he have anything in his hands?
A.	He had I think a razor, but I know he had a razor.
Q.	Did he have anything in his hand; did he have a razor in his hand?
A.	No sir, I didn't see nothing in his hand.
Q.	How do you know he had a razor?
A.	The reason that I said so he had a razor? He said so that he had a razor.[86]

Next the witness testified as to what was Honore's role in the case.

Q.	Did Honore say anything about this pistol when he comes in there?
A.	No sir, not while I was there. I did not hear him say anything about it.
Q.	Did you hear him say anything about the officer whether the officer was dead or not?
A.	Yes sir, he said the officer was dead. He said he was the one cut his throat to the high priest.
Q.	And the high priest is Davis?

---

[86] Ibid.

A.	Yes sir.[87]
Q.	He told him that he had cut the officer's throat?
A.	Yes sir.
Q.	From where you were standing outside of the gate, you couldn't see what was going on could you?
A.	No sir. I could see outside.
Q.	Did you see Honore have a dagger?
A.	No sir.
Q.	Did you ever see him with a dirk?
A.	No sir.
Q.	Did you see the officer draw his pistol?
A.	Yes sir.
Q.	Did you see anybody take it from him?
A.	No sir.
Q.	Did you see anybody throw him?
A.	I couldn't see, they had three men on him.
	Pierre questioning the witness Joseph Gasper.
Q.	Don't you remember that I was in the room sitting down with you?
A.	No sir, you were not, you were in the yard!
Q.	Weren't you in the room?
A.	You were in the yard I was in the room.
Q.	I went in the yard after.
A.	No sir, you were in the yard when it happen.
Q.	In the yard?
A.	Yes sir.
Q.	When the officer came there?
A.	No sir, when the officer throat was cut.[88]

This witness seemed confused. It appeared as though he wanted to convict Jack Pierre and Honore because the prosecution maintained they were guilty. He never saw what occurred in the yard. He never saw Honore cut the officer's throat or Jack Pierre holds him. He cleared Jack Pierre as the one who cut the officer's throat. He also makes the officer guilty of pulling his gun on Honore.

---

[87] Ibid., P.P. 11-12.
[88] Ibid.

The next witness was Dave Majors. He was a witness for the prosecution.

He was examined by Parker.

Q.   Now, that officer came to the gate, where were you when he came to the gate?

A.   Where was me? Well I was on the steps by the door.

Q.   When the officer came in the yard, who did you see out in the yard by the gate?

A.   Who did I see?

Q.   Yes.

A.   Ed Honore and that man.

Q.   Jack Pierre?

A.   Yes sir, Jack Pierre and Boyd, where is he at.

Q.   You mean Ferdinand Boyd?

A.   Ferdinand Boyd.

Q.   You don't mean old man Boyd do you?

A.   No sir.

Q.   Did you see him in the yard?

A.   Old man Boyd.

Q.   Yes

A.   Old man Boyd come out of the closet.

Q.   What did you see these men do to the officer?

A.   This man grabbed him.

Q.   Don't say this man, you mean Honore?

A.   Honore grabbed him and Jack Pierre and Boyd and shoved him out of the gate.

Q.   Did you see what happen after they had gotten him out of the gate?

A.   Sir

Q.   Did you see what happen after they had gotten him out of the gate?

A.   Well, then they took him by the neck and they held his neck and then I heard, gurgle, kind of noise like that, strangle.

Q.   Could you see from where you were standing exactly what they did?

A.   The cut was done.

Q.   You say those three men took hold of him?

A.   Yes sir, they took hold of him.

Q.   And they rushed him out of the gate?

A.   They rushed him out of the gate.

Q.   Did you see them throw him down?

A.   I never seen him thrown down.

Q.   You heard this gurgle?

A.   I heard that gurgle, yes sir.

Q.   And then where did you go?

A.	Where did I go?
Q.	After they cut the officer's throat?
A.	Then I went back inside and then they had a whole lot of white people.
Q.	Never mind now, don't go so fast on that. Were you in the room when Honore and Jack Pierre came back into the room?
A.	I was in the room when Honore and Jack Pierre come in the door.
Q.	After the officer was killed?
A.	Yes sir.
Q.	Did you see when Pierre came back there?
A.	Yes sir.
Q.	Did you see when Honore came back in the room?
A.	When Pierre comes back, yes sir, they came back in the room; we all came back in the room.
Q.	Did Honore have anything in his hands?
A.	I saw him with a dirk.
Q.	Did you see any pistol?
A.	He had the pistol; he had the officer's pistol.
Q.	Who had the officer's pistol?
A.	He had it in his hand.
Q.	Who?
A.	Ed Honore.
Q.	Mention his name?
A.	Ed Honore
Q.	Did Jack Pierre have anything in his hand?
A.	Jack Pierre, I didn't see him have anything in his hand; but I heard mention a razor, he had broke it.
Q.	Did you hear Honore say anything about the officer being dead?
A.	I never heard him say anything about him being dead. I heard him say that he cut his throat.
Q.	You heard Honore say that the he cut the officer's throat?
A.	The question was asked and he said I did it. Well done.
Q.	Who said well done?
A.	Honore.
Q.	Did you ever see Honore with any weapon?
A.	I seen him with the dirk.
Q.	What kind of dirk was it?
A.	It was sharpen on both ends.
Q.	What kind of handle did it have?
A.	If I ain't mistaken it had a kind of bone handle.
Q.	Where did you see the dirk?

41

A.   He had it in the middle wash stand there.[89]

The prosecution's next three witnesses established that the dirk found by Officer P. L. Tabarre was the one found at Honore's house. He also identified the officer's gun. Dr. A. L. Metrz established the fact that the dirk had human blood on it. The Coroner Dr. O'Hare established that the death of the officer was from a wound in the neck and that there was superficial cuts made by a razor.

At the conclusion of the Grand Jury trial the Judge directed questions to the accused as follows:

> You have any defense to make here? A. No, sir.
> By the court - you are entitled to take the stand and swear in your own behalf, both of you; but as you are not accompanied by an attorney, and I cannot appoint one for you, I would advise you not to make a statement at this time. You can do that in the higher court. By Mr. Parker - the State joins you, if your honor, please in that suggestion that they ought not to make a statement at this time.
> By the Court: You can make a statement if you want to, it would be better for you not to do it. But if you still insist upon doing it that is your privilege. But I would advise you not to make any statement at this time. Do you understand?
> By the accused: Yes sir.
> Committed to the Criminal District Court, without the benefit of bail.
> October 31st, 1907.
> A.M. Anacoin Judge. Second City Criminal Court.74[90]

The case was sent to trial after the Grand Jury indictment. The two accused were not aided by an attorney. An attorney was appointed for trial. Jack Pierre asked for a severance of his trial from that of Ed Honore. The actual trial of Ed Honore was set the 6th day of March 1908 at 10:30 o'clock a.m. The next chapter will be the actual trial of Honore and his appeal to the Louisiana

---

[89] Ibid., PP. 14 -16.
[90] Ibid., PP. 19 - 20.

Supreme Court.   The attorneys for Honore never presented a witness to determine if conflict in the testimony was planned or accidental.

Chapter III

The Trial of Edward Honore

Introduction:

"In Kentucky courts of law Negroes accused of a crime are being given eighteen minute trials and the latest was a ten minute trial with a mob outside the courtroom, twelve actual members of the mob in the jury box, a virtual member of the mob as judge, usually a confession extorted by torture in a back room before the trial, no defense whatever for the Negro victim/with the lack of defense concealed behind the presence of a so-called attorney for the victim, and a verdict of hanging delivered to the cheering mob from ten to eighteen minutes after the ceremony began."[91] This is not the trial I am about to relate in this thesis, but it gives an idea of the plight of Blacks during the era when the trial of Edward Honore took place. [70]

The only two men who had to face trial for the stabbing of officer Cambias were Honore and Pierre. The crime was committed on October 18, 1907. Pierre asked for a severance of his case from that of Honore's.   He was granted a separate trial. Edward Honore, the chief butler of the Council of God (C.O.G.) was called first. On January 30, 1908, at ten o'clock in the morning, Edward Honore faced the court to be tried for the killing of Robert J. Cambias, Jr. The jury was quickly impaneled and before five in the afternoon the district

---

[91] John Henrik Clark, <u>Marcus Garvey</u>, (New York: Vantage Books, 1974) 164.

attorney had his argument presented.[92] "The witnesses for the state were John Sherman, Ernest Bertonniers, Henry Boyd, and Dave Major. Their testimony coincided with the stories told at the time of the murder and with those of previous witnesses in the investigation. Judge H.D. Hollander was appointed by the court to defend him."[93] The attorney for Honore entered a self-defense plea. He based his defense on the fact that Cambias had drawn his gun on Honore. This should have been a good defense since any man who is in such a situation would try to protect his life. The attorney for Honore did not produce any witnesses to testify on behalf of Honore. The way things happened the others involved in the incident were shut up because of fear of prosecution. The first witness for the state was Dr. Joseph O'Hara.

Doctor Joseph O'Hara sworn statement follows. He was questioned by the District Attorney, Porter Parker.

> Q. You are the coroner for the Parish of Orleans?
> A. Yes sir.
> Q. Did you have on an occasion to hold an inquest on the body of a police office, Robert J. Cambias?
> A. Yes sir.
> Q. What did you find to be the cause of death?
> A. There was two deep incised wounds on the left side of the neck.
> Q. Will you point out those wounds?
> A. Deep incised wounds on the left side.
> Q. Could you tell whether these wounds were stab wounds or cut wounds?
> A. In my opinion, they were stab wounds.[94]
> Q. They began on the back portion of the neck, and extended forward around the neck as far as the thyroid carotid, on one, the second one, it began at the same place and it seemed to extend into

[92] W.P.A.,Dillon (Northwestern State University, Watson Memorial Library, Cammie G. Henry Research Center) folder 91 (103) 36.
[93] Ibid.,,. 36
[94] State vs. Honore: Criminal District Court for Parish of New Orleans, LA, P. 3.

the first wound, making one common wound, and then there was another superficial wound on the right side of the jaw.

    Is that correct?

A. Yes sir

Q. How about the superficial wound?

A. It looked more like a razor wound, when it cut into the second as a sharp blade the skin is always inverted and turned up.

Q. So, you say there were two wounds on the left side made by stab wounds, and one on the left side was made by a sharp instrument?

A. Yes sir.

Q. Could you tell which one of these wounds on the left side caused his death?

A. Yes sir, they severed all the muscles and caused external hemorrhaging.

Q. Was the body brought to the morgue?

A. Yes sir.

Q. It was there you held the autopsy?

A. Yes sir.

Q. Did you know officer Cambias yourself?

A. No sir.

Q. That was the first time that you saw him?

A. Yes sir.[95]

    The testimony of Dr. O'Hara was to establish the cause of death. Honore testified during the grand jury hearing that he cut the officer with a razor. Hollander did try to establish that Honore acted in self-defense. He could have pointed out that the Dr. had established that the razor cut did not kill the officer but the wounds made by another weapon caused the death of the officer. Now the Attorney for the defense question Dr. O'hara

    Q. Doctor, you speak of superficial wounds, you mean what?

A. One that does no damage.

Q. Were these superficial wounds made by the same instrument in your opinion as the two wounds on the opposite side?

A. No sir.

Q. What would a superficial wound show to the character of the instrument that made it?

A. It looked like a very sharp bladed instrument.

Q. This wound was on the right side?

A. Yes sir.

* Ibid.,,,, 2.

At this point in the proceeding, Parker questioned Dr. O'hara.

Q. Doctor did you see this weapon before?
A. Yes sir.
Q. Where did you get it?
A. It was turned over to the coroner's office, by some police officer.
Q. What did you do with it?
A. I myself turned it over to Professor Metz.
Q. Look at this razor and see if you ever had it in your possession.
A. Yes sir.
Q. Did you make the same disposition of that?
A. Yes sir.
Q. For what purpose?
A. For an investigation to see if there was any blood on it.

The defense attorney at this point conceited that there was human blood on the razor.

Then Parker continued.

We offer into evidence, four (4) photos marked S.1 to S.4 inclusive. We also, desire to offer into evidence, the place of the vicinity mark S.5.[96]

The next witness was Henry Boyd, the prosecution's star witness.

The following is the testimony of Boyd. The questioning was done by the District Attorney.

Q. Your name is Henry Boyd?
A. Yes sir.
Q. Were you a member of the Council of God?
A. Yes sir.
Q. What name were you known by in the Council of God?
A. Father Abraham.
Q. Do you know Honore, the man on trial?
A. Yes sir.
Q. How long did you know him?
A. Six or eight months.
Q. Was he a member of the Council of God?
A. Yes sir.
Q. By what name did he go?
A. The chief butler.
Q. Were you there the night that the officer came there?
A. Yes sir.[97]

---

[96] Ibld.,,.·3-4.
[97] Ibld.,,. 4

47

Q. Where were you at the time that the officer came to the place?
A. I was in the closet.
Q. Was the closet inside the yard?
A. The closet sets back in this direction.
Q. That was the closet just after you get into the yard?
A. No sir, it is about this distance from the gate, about from here to there.
Q. As you cam e into the yard on your right hand side is there an open shed?
A. Yes sir, a stable.
Q. And next to that is this close?
A. Yes sir.
Q. It was between the stable and the cistern?
A. Yes sir.
Q. Now did you see the officer come in the gate?
A. No sir, I didn't see him come in the gate.
Q. When did you first know that he was in the yard?
A. I didn't know that the officer was in the yard, I heard them talking. I didn't know that there was any officer in there, until I came out and I was buttoning up my pants, and then I saw the officer standing to my left up in the corner of the gate, and the gate opens, and he was up in the gateway talking to Honore, Pierre and Boyd.
Q. What did you see next?
A. When I came out I saw the officer have his pistol pointed at Honore. It looked as though he snapped it and then they grasped his arm, Boyd took one arm, and Honore got on top of him, and I heard him say, "Oh please don't kill me, please don't kill me", that is what the officer said.
Q. You say they backed him out of the gate?
A. Yes sir.
Q. How many of them had their hands on him?[98]
A. Two had their hands on him, one on each side, Boyd on the side next to the stable and Pierre was on the other side.
Q. What was Honore doing?
A. Honore was holding him.
Q. Did you see when he went to the ground?
A. Yes sir, I seen him when he went to the ground.
Q. What occurred when he went to the ground?
A. I saw them, they were working on him, say in this direction (illustrating) and I was nearly the distance of that?
Q. Who was working on his throat?
A. Honore.
Q. What was Pierre doing?
A. I didn't see Pierre do anything but stand on the side.

---

[98] Ibid.,,. 5.

Q. When they had hold of the officer and threw him down, what did you hear the officer say?
A. I heard him say "please don't kill me", and after that all I could hear was "ugh, ugh, ugh", choking like.
Q. After that what became of these three men, where did they go?
A. They went in the room where they were holding a meeting. Honore, Pierre, and Boyd.
Q. Did you go back in there?
A. Yes sir.[99]
Q. When Honore went back did he have anything else in his hands?
A. He had a revolver.
Q. Did he have anything else?
A. He had a revolver and a dirk.
Q. What sort of looking dirk was it?
A. Dirk with two pieces, one of these kinds of French dirks, horn handles yellowish like.
Q. Look at this dirk which I hand you and see whether this is the dirk he had or not?
A. That is the dirk.

At this point the state offered the dirk into evidence and Parker continued his questioning.

Q. Boyd when he went out of the gate did you hear them say anything about what they were doing to the officer?
A. I said to Pierre and Jack, you all have made a pledge not to kill; I said remember the sixth commandment.
Q. What did they say to you?
A. They never gave me no answer.
Q. After you all went back in the room where the meeting was held, what was done in there?
A. Well, when we went into the room, we commenced to sing.
Q. Did Honore say anything to you about what occurred on the street?
A. What had occurred?
Q. Yes, when you all got in the room, did Honore say anything to you about what had occurred in the street?
A. He said that he had cut his throat.
Q. Who did he say that to?
A. He said it to the High Priest.
Q. Who is the High Priest?
A. Sam Davis
Q. What did Davis say to him?
A. Well done.[100]

---

[99] Ibid.,,,., 6.
[100] Ibid.,,,., 8.

The defense attorney Hollander now cross-examine Boyd.

Q. What was the meeting there that night?
A. The Council of God.
Q. What was the Council of God?
A. It is a society all I know; better know as the Council of God.
Q. Was it gathered for the purpose of murder or killing or for the worship of God?
A. For the worship of God.
Q. How long had this society or sect been in existence?
A. A period of two years and six months, maybe more.
Q. How many times had they met in this place where this tragedy occurred?
A. I think they were there to my knowledge four or five times.
Q. Did they ever have any trouble with the police before?
A. No sir.
Q. They were peaceful and law abiding people?
A. Yes sir.
Q. You cannot be mistaken about anything that you have said?
A. No sir.
Q. You are sure that when you saw the officer walk into the yard that he had his pistol out and snapped it?
A. Yes sir.
Q. And Honore did not do anything at this time?
A. No answer.
Q. Was the officer in the yard when you saw him with his pistol in his hand?
A. Yes sir.[101]
Q. He pointed it at Honore and snapped it?
A. It looked as though he snapped it and then they grabbed him.
Q. Was Honore doing anything to him?
A. No sir.[102]

This is the end of Henry Boyd's testimony in this trial. The defense had established that the defendant did not act arbitrarily, but that the officer pulled and snapped his gun before Honore attacked him. O'hara established that there were superficial wounds caused by a razor. Honore admitted he used a razor and not the dirk on Cambias.

The next testimony is by John Sherman, the boy that was attacked prior to the killing of officer Cambias. The defense objects to the witness but was over

50

ruled by the judge. Only the portions of Sherman's testimony which the defense objected to will be presented. The defense objects on the grounds that a prior crime was relevant in the crime under examination.

> The following is the interchange between Parker and Sherman.
> Q. Where do you live?
> A. On Annette Street.
> Q. Do you know the prisoner Edward Honore?
> A. Yes sir.
> Q. Do you remember the night of the shooting down there? At the place of meeting of the Council of God?
> A. Yes sir.
> Q. Did you see Edward Honore there that night?
> A. Yes sir.
> Q. When was the first time you saw him and where did you see him?
> A. At the gate.
> Q. Did you see officer Cambias there that night?
> A. Yes sir.
> Q. Do you know Officer Cambias?
> A. Yes sir.
> Q. Where did you see Officer Cambias?
> A. At the drugstore.
> Q. How far is that from where you saw Honore?
> A. About four squares from there.
> Q. When you saw Officer Cambias, did you speak to him?
> A. Yes sir.[103]

The defense object to the testimony of Sherman as a witness, but the objection was over ruled and Parker continued his questioning.

> Q. Well, after this conversation did Officer Cambias go with you?

Holland then objected to any statement as to what Officer Cambias did with Sherman an hour before this incident occurred. The court overruled the objection and Parker continued his questioning.

> Q. Where did you go?
> A. I went to Honore's house.
> Q. Is that the place where you had seen Honore an hour before?

[101] Ibid.,,. 9.
[102] Ibid.,
[103] Ibid.,,. 10.

A. Yes sir.

Q. What occurred after you and Officer Cambias got to this place?

A. When I got there Officer Cambias asked me to point out the man.

Again defense objected: " We object to it, as anything that Officer Cambias did with regard to the commission of any other crime is not admissible by the court." [104]

The judge had the jury withdraw so that Holland could present his objection. The defense attorney objected that the meeting at the drug store between Cambias and Sherman was irrelevant. But the court overruled this objection. After the defense reserved a Bill of Exception (a Bill of Exception is a defense document that is meant to prohibit testimony by a witness in a court document to exclude the witness testimony from the court record) for this testimony. Parker continued his questioning.

Q. Now you lived in this neighborhood a number of years?

A. Yes sir.

Q. You were well acquainted with Ed. Honore?

A. Yes sir.

Q. How long did you know him?

A. I knew him by passing around this neighborhood.

Q. How long were you passing in this neighborhood?

A. Well as long as I can remember myself. [105]

The next witness for the State was E. Bertonnier who was examined by the district attorney.

Q. Where do you live?

A. I live on Lapegrouse St. for the present.

Q. Do you know where the defendant Honore lived?

A. Just about a block away.

Q. Do you know a young man named John Sherman?

A. Yes sir.

Q. On the 18th of October last at the time of this trouble did you see John Sherman earlier in the evening, did you see him?

A. No sir.

Q. Did you see Officer Cambias?

A. I saw him on the corner of Roman and New Orleans.

Q. What time was that?

A. That was about half past seven.

[104] Ibid.,,. 11.
[105] Ibid.,,. 15.

Q. Did you see when the officer went away form there?
A. That was the first time I saw him and that was with the boy.
Q. Who do you mean?[106]
A. Johnny and they went back they went two blocks away from there from where they met me. I met Cambias.
Q. What did you do and what did the Officer do?
A. The officer went in to the house into Honore's house, and I sat on the first step before you get to the house.
Q. Which way were you coming?
A. Coming from Claiborne Street.
Q. Were you going back down?
A. Yes sir.
Q. Is it down here? See if you understand this? (Explains map to witness off stand.)
Q. What occurred after you got there, Mr. Bertonnierre?
A. When I got there, the police told me he said.
At this point the defense objected and the objection was sustained by the court.

Q. State what occurred.
Defense makes the same objection that it is not admissible.
The court rules that it must be connected to the issue being discussed.
Q. You went there with the officer and John Sherman?
A. Yes sir.
Q. What occurred to Cambias or anyone else after you got there?[107]
A. We went into the place, Officer Cambias went into the place, he came out with Honore and his partner and when he got out of there these two men came from the back. Pierre and another man grabbed the policeman from the back and over powered him, and threw him down, and the only words he said was; Oh you Black son a bitches, that is the last words that I heard him say, and then they threw him down, when they got up they walked in the same door that they came out of, they then went and sang.
Q. What became of Cambias?
A. He was on the Banquette.
Q. Did you go to him?
A. No sir.
Q. You say that you stayed there for a half an hour?
A. Yes sir.
Q. Did you go to where Cambias was lying?
A. No sir.
Q. Now after you saw these men, one you recognized as Pierre, what did you say occurred?
A. They wrestled with him, and overpowered him and threw him down.[108]

---

[106] Ibid.,. 16
[107] Ibid.,. 16.
[108] Ibid.,. 17

53

Q. Did you see anyone do anything to him?"
A. The only man I say working his arm was Jack Pierre.
Q. How many of them had hold of him?
A. Three, Jack Pierre and one other.
Q. Who was the third man?
A. I don't know.
Q. Jack Pierre was one who was there?
A. Yes
Q. How many men were there?
A. Jack Pierre and Honore.
Q. And the third man you don't know?
A. No sir.

Hollander now cross-examine the witness.
Q. I understand you to say that you went and took a seat on the steps right near the gate?
A. Yes sir.
Q. And then you saw what you have related here happened?
A. Yes sir.
Q. Then you waited a half hour?
A. Yes sir.
Q. On the steps?
A. Yes sir.
Q. You never saw this officer move?
A. No sir.
Q. You never went away form there and gave any alarm?[109]
A. No sir.
Q. You stayed right there?
A. Yes sir, I could not do anything for him.

At this point in the proceeding there was a redirect by the prosecution.
Q. Who was this party you spoke of Tolman? Tolman, I don't know, no more than I can tell you that his name is John Tolman.
Q. You spoke to him?
A. I spoke to him first, he hit me on the shoulder and said; where is the officer?
The judge interjected and instructed the jury to ignore this last answer. Then the court said that this was no testimony and said the jury was not to consider the testimony.
Q. Did you ask Tolman to go anywhere?
A. Yes sir.
Q. You are sure of that?
A. Yes sir.
Q. Did Tolman come back?

[109] Ibid., 17.

"A. No sir, the corporal came back.
Q. The corporal of the police?
A. Yes sir.
Q. You stayed there until after he came?
A. Yes sir.[110]"

Dave Majors was now sworn in as a witness for the state. He was examined by the district attorney.
Q. Do you know Edward Honore?
A. Yes sir.
Q. How long did you know him?
A. I cannot commit it to memory.
Q. Were you a member of the Council of God?
A. Yes sir.
Q. And was Honore also a member?
A. Yes sir.
Q. Were you an ordained member, were you a full member, did you have a title? What was your name in the church and what were you know by?
A. I never went to no church.
Q. You were a member of the Council of God?
A. Yes sir.
Q. Did you have any name or title at the Council of God?
A. I had a name, they gave me prophet Micariah.
Q. What was Honore?
A. The Chief Butler.[111]
Q. Where were you the night that the police officer came?
A. I was there.
Q. His name was Cambias?
A. I don't know his name.
Q. You knew him by sight?
A. Yes sir.
Q. You knew him when you saw him?
A. Of course, he is dead.
Q. Where were you when the police officer came?
A. I was in the room and when the officer came to the room Honore ran out. And after Honore ran out, I came to the door and Pierre and Boyd.
Q. Where did Honore go?
A. Honore and Pierre went to the gate together.
Q. What did Pierre do?
A. Honore and Jack Pierre grabbed the officer.[112]
"Q. What happen then?
A. Honore cut him.
Q. Did you see him cut him?

---

[110] Ibid.
[111] Ibid., 18.
[112] Ibid.

55

A. I could not see him cut him, I was inside.

Q. When they grabbed the officer what did they do to the officer?

A. They shoved him out of the gate. Honore, Jack Pierre and Boyd.

Q. What became of the officer, did he keep his feet?

A. Honore and Jack Pierre, Honore said get out of here, and the officer drew his revolver, and that is the time that Ed. Honore and Boyd threw him out the gate, and Honore cut him, them words came from Honore's lips.

Q. Did you hear the officer make any sound?

A. The only thing I heard the officer say is like he had some one and they were about to choke him.

Q. What kind of sound?

A. Something likes a chicken when you wring its neck.[113]

Q. In other words you saw Pierre and Boyd and Honore shove him out the gate?

A. Yes sir, no sir, because I was inside but I can see as far as the gate.

Q. You said the officer said something about arrest?

A. The officer said I came to make an arrest?

Q. What did Honore say?

A. What do you want here, get out of here, the officer pulled his revolver, and that is the time that Honore grabbed him, and Jack Pierre and Boyd grabbed him.

Q. Now you say when he drew his pistol these three men grabbed him, Boyd, Pierre, and Honore. Now from the time that they grabbed him until the time you heard the gurgling sound, did these men keep hold of him?

A. I could not say.[114]

Q. Where did they go?

A. They went right inside the house.

Q. What did Honore have?

A. I say Honore have the dirk and the revolver of the policeman, if I am not mistaken. I think it is a kind of black pistol.

Q. Did Honore say anything?

A. He said that he killed him.

Q. Was it like that? The dirk.

A. It had a scabbard.

Q. Is this what you mean?

A. That is what I mean.

The prosecution then offered the scabbard as evidence.

Q. You were in the room when you heard this knocking on the gate?

A. Yes sir.

Q. Where was Honore?

A. He rushed out.

Q. Was he in the room too?

A. Yes sir, he was in the room.[115]

[113] Ibid.
[114] Ibid.,..19.

At this junction the defense attorney Hollander begins his cross-examination of Dave Majors.

Q. That was at Honore's?
A. Yes sir.
Q. That is where he resided, where he lived?
A. Yes sir.
Q. Do you know Henry Boyd?
A. Yes sir.
Q. Where was he at the time that the officer came there?
A. He had just come from the closet.
Q. He was nearer to these people than you were, and therefore he could see better than you could?
A. Yes sir.
Q. He stepped out just as the officer came out?
A. When these boys were arguing it was when he stepped out.[116]"

The next state witness was P. L. LeBarre.
"Q. Officer did you assist in the arrest of Honore?
A. No sir.
Q. Did you go down to the place where it is said that Honore lived?
A. Yes sir, about a half past ten.
Q. This night.
A. Yes sir.
Q. Did you make any examination of the premises when you got there?
A. Yes sir.
Q. Did you recover any weapons?
A. Yes sir, I found the dirk in the fireplace, and a .41 colt revolver between the springs in the bed.
Q. Do you know whose revolver it was?
A. No sir, I do not, it was a regulation .41 revolver.
Q. Is that the sort of pistol that is used by the police department?
A. Yes sir.[117]"

LeBarre testimony ended the states examination of witnesses. The only witness for the defense was Edward Honore who testified in his own behalf.

Defense attorney Hollander questioned Honore.
Q. What is your name?
A. Edward Honore.
Q. Where do you live?
A. They call it New Orleans Street.

---

[115] Ibid.,20
[116] Ibid.
[117] Ibid.

Q. How much do you weigh?

A. I used to weigh from 145 to 150 six or seven months ago.

Q. Were you a member of the society of the Council of God?

A. Yes sir.

Q. What was this society?

A. It was a bible society for the generation of Israel.

Q. Was there anything in the society or in its purpose other than the worship of God?

A. No sir.

Q. How long were you a member of it?

A. For the last six months as near as I can recollect.

Q. Tell this jury plainly and loudly how this killing took place, and what happened when this officer came to the gate?

A. The night when the killing took place, this here some boy he came here and he chunked some rocks."

At this point Parker objected to the whole testimony and said none of it should go to the jury.

Honore continues his testimony; "Well when the officer came I was sitting on the bed, he called me out. I came out, and from the distance of the door, I thought that he was going to ask me about this trouble, and when I go as far as the gate, I asked him what he was arresting me for, and he didn't lose no time, he take the revolver and he snaps it, and then I, I grabbed him and cut him".[118]

Q. What did you cut him with?

A. With a razor, a white handle razor.

Q. This is your razor?

A. Yes sir, it is my razor.

Q. Did anyone else jump on him?

A. Well there were two men out there, there was Latimore and Boyd, and then I took the revolver out of his hand and cut him.

Q. Was there any talk or any argument between the members of the Council of God to hurt anyone?

A. No sir.

Q. Then why did you cut this officer?

A. Because, I cut him to defend myself, because he snapped the gun at me.[119]

The district attorney, Parker, cross-examine Honore.

Q. Where was the officer when you first saw him?

A. At my door.

Q. At your gate or at your door?

---

[118] Ibid.,,. 21.
[119] Ibid., 22

A. At the door of my room.

Q. It was not at the outer gate?

A. Yes sir.

Q. He came all the way in the door of your room?

A. Yes sir, he called me out.

Q. Did you go out?

A. Yes sir.

Q. Where did you go?

A. I went as far as the gate.

Q. He told you, you were under arrest?

A. Yes sir.

Q. Where were Jack Pierre and Boyd?

A. They were inside the yard.

Q. Did they come with you?

A. I didn't see them, because they had their backs turned.

Q. When did you see them take hold of the officer?

A. I don't think they took hold of the officer until I got on the Banquette.[120]

Q. What did they do to him on the Banquette?

A. They must have __ they cut him.

Q. Did you see them throw him down on the Banquette?

A. Yes sir.

Q. Where were you when you saw them throwing him down?

A. I was going to the gate.

Q. You were outside on the Banquette?

A. Yes sir, when I took the revolver away.

Q. Boyd and Pierre were there?

A. I don't know whether Boyd was there.

Q. You say that you didn't have anything to do with it.

A. No sir.

Q. Now when the officer told you that you were under arrest you say this was at your door?

A. Yes sir.

Q. Why did he draw the pistol, you were going along with him, were you not?

A. Because I asked him why are you arresting me? He didn't say anymore.

Q. Is that all you said?

A. Yes sir.

Q. And after that he drew his pistol, and tried to shoot you?

A. Yes sir.

Q. Where did you get your razor?

A. I had it here.

Q. Where did you get your razor from when you cut him?

A. I had it in my vest pocket (illustrating).

---

[120] Ibid.

Q. He drew the pistol on you?
A. Yes sir.
Q. You didn't draw this razor until you got to the gate?
A. Until he drew the revolver, yes sir and snapped it.
Q. Did he try to snap it again?
A. I didn't give him a chance.
Q. Now isn't it a fact that the officer didn't draw his pistol on you until you all drew weapons on him?
A. He drew it on me.
Q. How near to you was Boyd and Pierre at the time you say he drew his revolver?
A. Right about the stable door, they were at the stable door.
Q. What were they doing there?
A. They were standing up there.
Q. Did they follow?
A. I never notice, I had my back turned.
Q. Now you do know when they got to the gate they were there?
A. Yes sir.
Q. They must have got to the gate?
A. I suppose.
Q. Now when you cut the officer with the razor you went back into the room?
A. Yes sir.
Q. You stayed there long enough to cut the officer and see them throw him down?
A. Yes sir.
Q. Now do you know who killed the officer?
A. Well, I could not really say because I didn't take notice. [121]
Q. When you came back into the room where the apostle was, did you tell him anything in regard to this?
A. No sir.
Q. The wound you made was the razor cut?
A. Yes sir.
Q. Now when you came back into the room, how is it you had this dirk in your hand?
A. No sir.
Q. All men of your society, who say you had the dirk in your hand. They are not telling the truth?
A. They are saying something that I did not have.
Q. Whose dirk is that?
A. It was at my house, someone who was working on a ship left it there, it was in my washstand drawer, and I never took it out.
Q. Did Boyd or Pierre know that you had it?
A. Boyd used to take it out. [122]

[121] Ibid., 23.
[122] Ibid.

Q. Did the officer fall when you cut him?
A. No sir.
Q. Did you see either of the others with a weapon?
A. I didn't see them, but I know they had them.[123]"

This ended the testimony in the Edward Honore trial. The defense then filed

an appeal to the Louisiana Supreme Court. The testimony in this trial was

conflicting. Honore admitted that he cut the officer but maintained this was not

the wound that killed the officer. If the defense could have proved that Honore

was assaulted without cause or provocation by Cambias, then he would not

have been guilty of the crime charged. In that case he could have only been

found guilty of manslaughter. But Hollander failed in the effort to claim self-

defense and the jury found Honore guilty of murder.[124] It also appeals by the bill

---

[123] Ibid.,,. 24.

The Appeal

NO. 17409
Supreme Court of Louisiana filed March 23, 1908
State of Louisiana vs. Edward Honore and Jack Pierre

Appealed from the Criminal District Court, section vs. Judge F.Q.
presiding. The Attorney General for the State of Appeals Henry D.

of exception that the defendant asked for a new trial on the ground of newly discovered evidence. The court stated that the grounds were not found to be sufficient to set aside the verdict. The ruling of the court regarding them was not in error.

> It was for the jury to determine under proper instructions whether the facts were such as to render it evident that the defendant was guilty. Thus, the defendant did this and it now remains for the court to consider the question of law and such facts properly brought up before the court as may be needful in considering these questions.[125]

The Appeal

NO. 17409
Supreme Court of Louisiana filed March 23, 1908
State of Louisiana vs. Edward Honore and Jack Pierre

Appealed from the Criminal District Court, section vs. Judge F.Q. presiding. The Attorney General for the State of Appeals Henry D. Hollander and B.B. Howard for the Defendant, appellant Honorable J. Porter Parker District Attorney for the State.

Briefs were filed on behalf of Appellant Edward Honore for rehearing. Appeal form the Criminal District Court, Parish of Orleans.

On the seventh day of November 1907 the grand jury found a true bill against the defendant, charging him with having taken the life of Robert J. Cambias, on the 18th of October 1907.

He was arraigned and in January he was placed on trial and on the 31st day on the month he was found guilty of murder as charged.[124]

The defendant having no counsel was defended by a court appointed lawyer who appealed to this court from the verdict found by the jury and the sentence of the court.

There was a bill of exceptions in the record setting out the different grounds of defense, such as that the verdict is contrary to the law of evidence. That the verdict failed to give to the accused the benefit of such reasonable doubt as he was entitled to under the law; that the court charged the jury that if the accused submitted to arrest.

[125] Ibid.,. 2-3.

The only point argued before the court in the brief on appeal is whether the evidence of a separate and distinct offense is admissible although not connected with the offense charged.

The facts are as relates to this point that one hour before the commission of the crime charged, at a distance of about five squares from the scene of the homicide, a witness, John Sherman, who had been wounded in the neck and back, was at a drug store where he was having his wounds dressed. The deceased Cambias who was in uniform and on duty, entered the drug store and spoke to this witness, and the witness, Sherman, at that time told him how he had received his wounds. The witness left the drug store in company with the police officer and repaired to the place where he had been wounded and pointed out the defendant as his assailant.

We have noted that the officer having received information sufficient to put him upon inquiring attempted to make the arrest as was proper for him to do if he had reason to believe that the facts were such as stated to him by the witness. How better to prove that the officer had seen the wounded man, and there upon went to the scene of the homicide and attempted to effect the arrest when he was killed.

The purpose of the District Attorney is using Sherman, as a witness was not to prove to the jury that another crime had been committed, but to prove why it was that the officer sought to make the arrest. This court has laid down the rule that a police officer may prove why it was that he sought to make an arrest or made an arrest and that he was in the discharged of the duty with which he was entrusted as an officer.[126]

The lower court proved that this witness, Sherman, was not to prove to the jury that another crime had been committed but to prove why it was that the officer sought to make the arrest. The court cited two cases, State vs. Denkins, 24A. 29; and State vs. Stouderman, 6A., 288. The court said that this appeal was different because there was no purpose to prove another crime not connected with the cause for which the accused was tried. The testimony related to the cause for which an attempt was made to arrest the accused. The court found the testimony was admissible under the authorities that were cited.[127]

The purpose of the charge was, this court inferred to direct the attention of the jury to the fact that the purpose in admitting the testimony was that they might consider the motive of the deceased officer at the time of the homicide and that it was not a wanton or illegal attempt to arrest the accused. The court considered the different questions raised and the

[126] Ibid.,,. 4-5.
[127] Ibid.,,. 8.

result is as before expressed. The court does not think that they should change the verdict and the sentence from the grounds argued. It follows that the court must affirm the judgment.

For reasons stated, it is ordered adjudged and decreed that the judgment appealed from be and same is hereby affirmed.[128]

This is the end of the trial of Edward Honore. The counsel for Honore should have presented the issue of self-defense and cited the statements of Boyd and Majors as evidence that Honore acted to defend himself when the officer pulled his revolver and snapped it at Honore. Honore's testimony coincided with that of both witnesses. Honore did admit that he cut the officer with a razor and the doctor affirmed that the wound made by the razor was superficial and not fatal. The appendices will contain detailed information on the appeal.

---

[128] Ibid.. 9.

Chapter IV

The Trial of Jack Pierre

The trial of Jack Pierre was drawn out because of the cross-examination of the Defense Counsel. The defense attorney attempted at the end of the trial to prove that Pierre was insane which resulted in a guilty verdict against Jack Pierre. The Defense also accused the two principle witnesses of the state of being lunatics. This was based or the claim by Dave Majors and Henry Boyd that they were reincarnations of Biblical characters. Both men swore that they had lived before in many different bodies. The defense in its cross-examination questioned each as to their belief in transmigration of their souls. In the Bill of Exception the defense attorney used two arguments. Primarily that the Grand Jurors were drawn from an unconstitutional body of Jury Commissioners; the members of this Jury commissioners were appointed by the Governor of the state; that the Governor is without constitutional authority to appoint jury commissioners, that it was decided by the supreme court of the state. Also, the appointment of jury commissioners was a judicial and not an executive function.[129]

During the trial of Jack Pierre the defense cross-examined the witnesses extensively. Indeed a juror stood up and objected to this attempt of the defense to prove the witnesses, Majors and Boyd were insane. The defense further questioned the integrity of the state witnesses, Sherman and Bertonnierre. The

---

[129] State of Louisiana vs. Jack Pierre "Criminal District Court", Parish of Orleans Section B. 1908- p.1.

charge against Sherman's reliability was based or the defense contention that he lied about being a Negro. According to Pierre's defense Sherman also lied to Cambias. He testified that he did see who attacked Cambias, although he was two feet from him when the incident occurred. Bertonnierre was questioned as to why he stood by and watched Cambias being assaulted and did nothing to help him. He was accused of being a coward by the defense.[130]

This study will now proceed to provide a portion of the testimony of the witnesses in this case and will give a synopsis of the states questions and the major points of the cross-examination by the defense lawyer William H. Luzenberg.

The defense drew up a bill of exception in this case, which will be included in the appendix. The appendix will also include the findings of the State Supreme Court. Because of the length of the cross-examination of the witnesses by the defense. This chapter will provide only the main points of the defense. There will be only small excerpts from the critical testimony of Jack Pierre and Sam Davis. But they will be more extensive than the other testimony because of their value in bringing to bear new facts in this trial.

The first witness for the state was Dr. O'Hara. Dr. O'Hara testified that the cause of death in this case was two deep wounds on the left side of the neck.

> Well there were two wounds, one of them began on the upper side of the neck on the left side of the vertebrate column, and then there was one around here in the neck by the Adam's apple, severing all of the muscle arteries. Then there was another one

---

[130] Ibid., p. 2.

about half an inch in length, starting in the back,
coming back and making one common wound.[131]

Dr. O'Hara stated that two weapons could have inflicted the wounds. He
identified the murder weapon as being a heavy instrument, which caused death.
The other wounds were inflicted by a razor because they were inverted. On
cross-examination the doctor was asked whether the wound that caused the
death of Cambias was the wound that pierced the back of the neck, cutting the
throat. He answered in the positive and was then asked if the wounds could
have been inflicted after death. He replied definitely not, and also testified that a
sharp blade, such as a razor inflicted the superficial wound.

> The next witness for the State was Henry Boyd. At this point the
> State in evidence a diagram of the premises where the murder
> occurred.

The District Attorney Parker asked Boyd where he was the night of the
incident. Boyd stated he was in the water closet and testified that he knew Pierre
and Honore. He also testified that he was a member of the Council of God. The
District Attorney asked him what happened the night that the officer came to the
house.

> Q. Now when the officer came there state what happened?
> A. When the officer first came there, I was inside of the closet. I
> heard them talking. I heard the officer say fall in, you are my
> prisoner and Apostle Paul said don't you do it.
> Q. That is the one called Apostle Paul?
> A. Yes sir, I came out, and I was buttoning up my pants, I heard
> him say don't you do it, and then the officer took his gun out and
> pointed it and the gun snapped and then Pierre grabbed one arm
> and Boyd the other and Honore grabbed him and they backed him

---

[131] Ibid., p. 4.

out of the gate, and with that I saw Honore was on top of him cutting him, and I heard him say, please don't kill me.[132]

The district attorney asked him who were the three parties that had hold of Cambias. Boyd named Pierre and a young fellow named Boyd along with Honore. He testified that Honore cut the officers throat and that Pierre was an eyewitness that saw everything that happened. Then he was asked what happened when he went back into the House.[133]

> Q. After you went back into the room; did Honore, Boyd and Pierre come back into this room?
> A. They came into the room and Honore came in with the revolver in his hand, and he said there is one lead out of it, he said one chamber is empty, he said it was empty when he got it, the laid the revolver on the bed, and they told the high priest, what they had done.
> Q. What did Honore say?
> A. Honore said I killed him.
> Q. What did Pierre say?
> A. I never heard him say anything.[134]

The district attorney asked him what Pierre had in his hands. Boyd responded that Pierre had a razor and that he only saw the blade of the razor and could not tell what kind of handle it had. Boyd also said that Honore had a dirk. Parker then showed him the dirk and Boyd said that it was the dirk he had seen Honore with that night. Parker then offered the dirk as evidence.[135]

Boyd was cross-examined by the defense attorney William Luzenberg. Luzenberg asked Boyd about his eyes. Boyd said that he had to wear spectacles because of a cataract in his eye. Luzenberg referred to him as uncle.

---

[132] Ibid., p.5.
[133] Ibid., p.7.
[134] Ibid., p.8.
[135] Ibid.

He asked Boyd what they called him in the church and he responded that they called him Father Abraham. Luzenberg questioned Boyd about the razor Pierre had and the dirk Honore had. He also asked how far was he from them. Boyd responded that he was about 7 feet away.[136] Luzenberg also questioned him about the color of the razor's handle.

> Q. I understand you to say that you could not see what color the handle was?
> A. I hadn't mentioned the razor.
> Q. Did you see anyone with the razor?
> A. Pierre had the razor.
> Q. He had it in his hand?
> A. Yes sir.
> Q. And the District Attorney asked you what kind of handle it was?
> Q. I said I could not tell what kind of handle it had; I only saw the blade.
> Q. Can you see the blade of the razor?
> A. Yes sir.
> Q. That is the same blade you saw this night, right?
> No answer.
> Q. It looks like the blade you saw that night.[137]

Luzenberg asked Boyd if he saw the dirk and could he swear to it being the same one in Honore's possession. Luzenberg then began to question Boyd about his religious convictions. He asked him about what Boyd apparently had said about Jesus Christ, if he had once said that if Jesus were on earth near him he would cut his throat. Boyd replied that things had changed and that he was not as dictatorial as he had once been. Luzenberg then asked Boyd was he leading a pious religious life, and about what churches he had joined. Boyd

---

[136] Ibid , p. 10.
[137] Ibid.

69

replied that he had been Methodist and Baptist before becoming a member of the Council of God.[138]

Luzenberg questioned Boyd further about his religious belief. Boyd testified that he was the same spirit that existed two thousand years ago as Father Abraham. He was asked to describe the career of Abraham in the Bible. In this regard, Luzenberg asked Boyd about Abraham's concubines and how many wives he had. Boyd stated that he was the same identical Abraham in a different body, but he was not a different spirit. His body was different but his spirit was the same. He had but one wife and her name was Sarah. Luzenberg then asked Boyd if he would swear that his spirit was the spirit of Abraham that existed two thousand years ago. He answered "yes sir". Continuing his questioning Luzenberg asked Boyd if he was the same Abraham who died two thousand years ago and what did he do in the years after Abraham's death. Boyd stated,

> In this world, first I was a Chinamen, then after I was a Greek and then a nigger. I was a nigger; I was a nigger from the foundation of the world. I am in my seventy-fifth body now.[139]

The lawyer then asked Boyd when he was first born. His reply was, "he could not say". And then when asked about his second body Boyd answered, "he could not say".[140]

The state at this point introduced an expert on the weather. Dr. Lindsay Kline testified that it was a clear night on October 18, 1907. Luzenberg

---

[138] Ibid., p. 11 & 12.
[139] Ibid., p. 23-24.
[140] Ibid.

questioned the doctor on the visibility on that night. The doctor said he could not, and that only an expert could tell. Luzenberg asked if sometimes Dr. Kline made mistakes. Kline stated that the weather bureau never made predictions about the weather or moon. They only observed if the moon was clear or not. Luzenberg noted that the doctor had stated that the moon was clear up to midnight.[141]

The next witness was John Sherman, the boy who was attacked by Honore and Pierre the night of October 18, 1907. Sherman was a witness for the state. He was first questioned by Parker; the district attorney. When asked whether he knew Jack Pierre, he stated he did for about seven years. Parker asked him if he saw Pierre the night of the murder. Sherman stated that he had seen Pierre the night of the murder. The District Attorney asked Sherman if he passed Honore's house on the night of October 18, 1907. Sherman responded that he passed there about eight o'clock and was stopped by Honore.[142]

Parker then asked John Sherman to tell the jury what happened to him. I was passing Honore's house about half-past eight, when Honore asked me what I meant, he said you know what I mean, and he started to cut at me. And when I got within thirty feet of the gate Jack Pierre caught hold of me and kicked me and punished me, and I went to the drugstore and got my wounds dressed. When we got to Honore's house he asked me to point out the men who cut me. I pointed them out. I pointed out Jack Pierre to go around. Then I got out of the

---

[141] Ibid., p. 25.
[142] Ibid., p. 27.

way and went around by the gate. And then I heard them holler. I heard Cambias holler, "Oh", and then I started to run.[143]

The District Attorney questioned Sherman whether he saw Honore and Jack Pierre do anything to Cambias. He replied, "no sir", Parker, these asked Sherman if he had returned later that night. Sherman responded that when he returned he saw Cambias on the ground dead and that there was blood near him. The witness further stated that he saw Cambias near the banquette, and that Ernest Bertonnierre was present as well as two other officers who had arrived to arrest Honore and Pierre.[144]

The cross-examination of John Sherman by the defense attorney, Luzenberg, began after Parker had finished questioning with the witness. Responding to Luzenberg examination, Sherman stated that after he was cut he went to the drugstore and met officer Cambias. He also said that he accompanied Cambias to Honore's house and that he went inside the gate. He was then asked what kind of night it was. Sherman replied that is was a clear moonlight night. Luzenberg stated that he would not try to confuse the witness but was seeing the truth. Sherman responded that he knew Pierre for seven years.

The witness was then caught the in a contradiction by Luzenberg because he had stated in Honore's trial that the officer came outside the gate, but in his present testimony he said that the officer did not come outside.[145]

---

[143] Ibid., p. 27-28.
[144] Ibid., p. 29.
[145] Ibid., p. 32.

The defense attorney asked Sherman about what occurred as he saw it.

> Q. In the other court do you remember being asked did you see what happened, do you remember what occurred?
> A. Yes sir.
> Q. Did you see what occurred?
> A. Yes sir.
> Q. In the other court what made you say no if you said no?
> A. No sir.
> Q. You didn't see what occurred then?
> A. No sir.
> Q. Did you see what made officer Cambias holler?
> A. No sir.
> Q. You heard him holler, and you ran?
> A. Yes sir.
> Q. You did not see what occurred then?
> A. No sir.[146]

Luzenberg asked Sherman who he saw put their hands on Cambias. The witness stated that he did not see anyone put their hands on the officer. He also stated that there were two other men with Honore and Pierre and that they were between Honore and Pierre. When Sherman was asked whether the two men were closer to Cambias than Honore and Pierre, he gave no answer. He later said that Honore was the closest to Cambias. Sherman testified that he did not see the trouble that occurred that night. He also testified that he was two feet from the gate and about five feet from Cambias, but did not see anything.[147] This portion of the testimony follows:

> Q. What I am trying to get from you is that you are telling the truth as far as you know it?
> A. Yes sir.
> Q. Where was Pierre?
> A. Towards the back.
> Q. How far back of these men was he?
> A. They were all in line.

---

[146]Ibid., p. 33.
[147]Ibid., p. 34-35.

Q. Five feet, ten feet?

A. That is about as far as the whole bunch was that was there five feet away.

Q. He was nearest to Honore or Pierre?

A. Honore was nearest to him and when he called to him he came to him.

Q. How long were you out of the gate, before you heard anything else?

A. As soon as I backed out of the gate I heard him holler.

Q. How far you had to walk to get out of the gate?

A. Just about two feet and then I was out of the gate.[148]

Luzenberg asked Sherman if he saw Bertonnierre when he ran for help. Sherman responded that Bertonnierre was hiding by the steps and that he was a cripple and could not run. Sherman also stated that he heard Officer Cambias tell Honore and Pierre they were under arrest and then Officer Cambias hollered. He also stated the only thing he heard was the officer say, "oh".[149]

This witness was caught in contradictions by the defense. The next witness, Bertonnierre, was questioned by the defense and was accused by the prosecution of being a coward. He was sitting on a step a few feet away and watched Cambias being killed and never tried to stop the people attacking the officer. His testimony was conflicting too. The defense in their bill of exceptions accused him of telling a thousand lies.

The state then offered in evidence, a sketch of the premises. Ernest Bertonnierre was sworn in for the State and then examined by the District Attorney, Parker. The witness was examined by the responding to Parker's questioning. Bertonnierre stated that he knew Honore, but did not know Officer Cambias. He maintained that the first time he saw the officer he was with the

---

[148] Ibid., p. 34-35.

boy John Sherman. Bertonnierre stated that he went with the officer and John Sherman until they reached the first box step from New Orleans Street and that after he got there he saw the officer and the young fellow, he went there and he said to the boy, who cut you, and the boy said, Jack Pierre and Honore. Then another man, who he did not know, grabbed the officer and threw him down. He said that the only words he heard the officer say was, "you black son of a bitches" and that was all he said.[150] Bertonnierre, the witness was confused.

When Parker asked the witness, Bertonnierre, about the two men who came out the yard with Officer Cambias as his prisoners, he responded that it was Ed. Honore. The witness was then asked about what occurred in the yard.

> Q. Did anyone else follow him out?
> A. Two men Jack Pierre and another man.
> Q. Do you know who the other man was?
> A. No sir.
> Q. Now what occurred after they threw the officer down?
> A. They did whatever they wanted to, and they went inside and then they went back and sang.
> Q. Did you hear them singing?
> A. I stayed in the same place where I was.
> Q. Did the officer get up?
> A. No sir.
> Q. Did anyone come in this place?
> A. Only one man, Johnny Tolman, came and asked me where the policeman was. I said he is laying down about 11 feet away form me, and I stayed in the same place. I had just had a paralytic stroke and I could not get about, as I wanted to.
> Q. What became of Tolman?
> A. He left there.[151]

Bertonnierre was asked by Parker to identify the man who threw the officer down.

[149] Ibid., p. 37.
[150] Ibid., p. 40-41.

Q. From these steps could you see well enough to identify the men who had hold of Cambias?

A. Yes sir.

Q. And you are positive that one of the men who threw him down was Jack Pierre the defendant?

A. Yes sir.

Q. And one was Honore?

A. Yes sir.

Q. And the other man?

A. I don't know who he was.

Q. Did you ever see him before?

A. No sir.

Q. That is what you mean?

A. Yes sir.

Q. While they had hold of Officer Cambias and was throwing him down, could you see what they were doing?

A. The only man I say was Jack Pierre, he was working his arm, but I didn't see what he was doing.[152]

Bertonnierre was next cross-examined by the defense attorney.

Luzenberg who asked the witness about his position near the steps and

whether he had talked to anyone about he case.

Q. Have you discussed it with anyone at all?

A. No sir.

Q. In any gas rooms or any other place?

A. No, sir, but what I am telling right now.

Q. You were sitting on the steps?

A. By the steps.

Q. Were you hiding?

A. No sir. The light was facing the other way, and I was in the dark, so that they could not see me at all.

Q. You were there?

A. Yes sir.

Q. Did you see the boy by the name of Sherman?

A. Sure, he went there with the officer, afterwards I didn't see him.[153]

---

[151] Ibid., p. 41.

[152] Ibid., p. 42.

[153] Ibid., p. 43.

The defense questioned Bertonnierre about the position of Sherman. Bertonnierre testified that he was near the gate and also stated that Sherman never passed him but he did see a Negro pass him. He then stated it was not a moonlight night and that it was a dark night. He maintained that if the electric light on the corner had not been there it would have been "pitch dark". When asked if the electric light had not been shinning, he could not have seen to the gate, he replied that it would not had been so dark to see to the gate.[154]

Bertonnierre contradicted himself several times in his testimony.

Q. You say you didn't see Sherman go past near where you were?
A. No sir, I didn't pay any attention, I didn't see anyone come in the back.
Q. You say Cambias come out of the gate with the prisoner?
A. Yes sir.
Q. He didn't come out by himself?
A. No sir.
Q. Your intention is to stick to what you said?
A. Yes sir, I didn't see anything false, this is all the truth.
Q. Did you notice anything in Honore's hands?
A. No sir, in none of their hands.
Q. I understand you to say a few moments ago that you say Jack Pierre hands work up and down?
A. Yes sir.
Q. If it attracted your attention in such a manner you ought to be able to know which arm it was.
A. I was so excited I could not tell you which arm it was.
Q. You were arrested yourself Mr. Bertonnierre have you not been?
A. Oh, yes, several times for simple charges.[155]

Luzenberg challenged Bertonnierre's ability to observe to incident.

Q. You didn't see Honore move his arm?
A. No sir.
Q. If he had moved his arms could you have seen it?
A. No sir, I don't believe I could.
Q. If this third man had moved his arm could you have seen him?

---

[154] Ibid., p. 46.
[155] Ibid., p. 48.

A. No sir, I don't believe I could.
Q. If Jack Pierre moved his arms could you have seen him?
A. Well, I could at this time.[156]

These were the main points of the testimony of Bertonnierre.

The last witness for the State was Dave Majors. All these witnesses had previously testified in the case of Ed Honore. The defense successfully identified points in their answers that conflicted with their testimony in the Jack Pierre trial.

Majors, the next witness for the state, was questioned by Parker. Majors stated that he, Honore, Pierre, and Boyd all were inside the house when the officer came. He stated that Honore, Pierre and Boyd rushed out. When the officer came to the gate, Majors testified that he sat at the door on the sill and that he saw Honore take out the dagger from a table drawer and then rush to the gate.[157] The transcript of Majors' testimony follows:

Q. Can you see the gate from where you were standing?
A. Right on the sill of the door.
Q. By the steps?
A. And I looked directly to the gate.
Q. That is right in line with the gate?
A. Yes sir.
Q. Now tell what happened?
A. Honore, Jack Pierre and Boyd, grabbed the officer and shoved the officer out of the gate, and I saw Jack Pierre with razor, and I saw Honore with the pistol and the dirk.
Q. And Pierre.
A. Pierre had the razor.
Q. When did you see the razor?
A. That time that the trouble occurred after the officer was killed I saw him with a razor, and I just saw the blade.[158]

---

[156] Ibid., p. 49
[157] Ibid., p. 51.
[158] Ibid., p. 52.

Majors testified that when Pierre came back inside the room he had a razor and Honore a dirk and a revolver, presumably the officer's revolver. He said that Pierre admitted he killed the officer. Majors said that Daniel Latimore asked who killed the officer and said, "well done".

Majors was asked by Parker whether he saw the dagger anytime before that night and he replied "no". When asked did he see it anytime before, except when Boyd brought it back in the room, he also responded "no".

> Q. Did you ever see it at any other time?
> A. The first time I saw it.
> Q. Before that did you ever see it before?
> A. I never seen it any other time but that night.
> Q. You didn't see it at any other time except when Boyd brought it back in the room?
> A. Yes sir.

The witness also said he had not seen the dagger at the house, except the night when Honore grabbed it from a table drawer and rushed out. He maintained that Pierre followed Honore.[159]

Parker then asked Majors what had occurred in the yard.

> Q. Now after Honore had gotten this dagger, and got out in the yard, what occurred out in the yard, what did you see, tell the jury exactly what you saw?
> A. I saw Jack Pierre, Honore and Boyd at the gate.
> Q. What did they do?
> A. Honore and the officer were talking and the only thing that I heard Honore say was I ain't going anywhere, and then he said get out of here.
> Q. And then he said get out of here?
> A. Yes sir.
> Q. Who did he say that to?
> A. To the officer and at this time Jack Pierre and Francis Boyd, grabbed him, and shoved him out of the gate, I could not tell you what happen because I never was at the gate.[160]

---

[159] Ibid., p. 54.

Luzenberg then cross-examined Majors who asked the witness that Sam Davis has boosted that it would take forty policemen to take him out of the house.

Majors was then questioned about being in jail and testifying in the Honore case.[161] Majors complained the defense was that trying to put him Majors in a hole and let Jack Pierre off. Luzenberg questioned him about that.

> Q. Now if anyone else says different you are not telling the truth, you are mistaken.
> A. They may try to put me in the hole.
> Q. You don't want to be put in the hole?
> A. Yes sir, according to my knowing.
> Q. That is why you are testifying?
> A. Yes sir.[162]

Luzenberg questioned Majors about his religious beliefs and about the Council of God.

> Q. What are you in the Council of God?
> A. I am a prophet that was my birthright, from the foundation of the world; the law was written down and handed to Moses. It is in the 20th Chapter.
> Q. How do you know it is in the 20th chapter?
> A. The 20th Chapter of Exodus. I say this was my birth right name at the beginning of the world.[163]

Majors was questioned by Luzenberg about his statement that he had existed since the foundation of the world.

> Q. You don't mean to say you had a name at the foundation of the world?
> A. Yes sir.
> Q. Were you born then?
> A. Yes sir.

---

[160] Ibid., p. 54.
[161] Ibid., p. 55.
[162] Ibid., p. 57.
[163] Ibid., p. 59.

Q. How old are you?
A. Thirty-one years old, born in 1877.
Q. What is your name in the Council of God?
A. Prophet Melciah.
Q. How old is the prophet Melciah?
A. Just go backward and forward, reincarnation.
Q. How many times have you been born?
A. I am in my seventy-fourth body?
Q. That is as true as everything else you have said?
A. Yes sir.[164]

This ended Dave Majors' testimony. He was the last witness for the state.

The next two witnesses for the defense were Sam Davis and Jack Pierre. The

court instructed Davis in this case that you were charged as being an accessory

after the fact.[165]

The court wants to put you on your guard that anything you say will be

used against you. The witness was questioned by Luzenberg, for the defense

who also advised Davis not to answer questions that would incriminate him.[166]

Q. Your name is Sam Davis?
A. Yes sir.
Q. You understood what the judge told you?
A. Yes sir.
Q. Sam, what we are trying to get at is the truth, you are not to tell
anything that may incriminate you in anyway, if I ask you
anything that will incriminate you don't answer it. If there is
anything that I ask you that will hurt you, you don't have to
answer it? Where do you live?
A. 2325 Lawarpe Street.[167]

The witness, Sam Davis, was asked about the service that was being held

the night the trouble began. Luzenberg asked was Davis if there was any

interruption that night to the service. Davis responded that there were 14

---

[164] Ibid., p. 59.
[165] Ibid.
[166] Ibid.

interruptions. He was also asked if he sent anyone out to see who was throwing

rocks at the house and interrupting the meeting. He stated that he sent Honore

out, and that Boyd and Latimore also went out. Davis testified that Pierre was at

the door inside, and that he did not remember him going out and that Pierre was

sitting at the door. Davis said that Pierre was the first to return.[168]

Davis was questioned about the locating of Jack Pierre when the other

men were in the yard.

> Q. Where was Jack Pierre?
> A. Sitting at the door inside and while they were there talking of course I could hear a voice, I know from the sound of the voice that they were not out in the street that is the reason that I say they were in the yard.
> Q. How did you call them?
> A. I said to brother Pierre, I said you call the brothers, and let me know something, the only thing that I could hear was that someone was lying on the Banquette and I said go and call those brothers up there quick, he steps outside the door and called them, and I said how many brothers are there and he said there are four out there.
> Q. Who were the four?
> A. There was Paul.
> Q. Who is Paul?
> A. Paul, Latimore, Edward Honore, Ferdinand Boyd and Jasper.
> Q. What is Jasper's other name?
> A. Joseph Jasper, he said, Are all of the brothers there; and I called for the old man.[169]

Davis stated that the men looked a little scared when they came in. He

also testified that Latimore was the one who said, "well done". Davis said that he

asked the brothers' questions about what had happened, but they would not tell

---

[167] Ibid.

[168] Ibid., p. 60.

[169] Ibid., p. 68.

him anything about the incident in the yard. He said that Latimore, Young, Boyd and Honore looked scared when they came back in the house.[170]

The witness, Sam Davis, was cross-examined by Parker for the state. Davis was asked who went out and, most specifically, when did Jack Pierre go out.

Q. Who did you send out, Honore?
A. Yes sir.
Q. Did anyone else go?
A. Yes sir.
Q. Who?
A. There was David Latimore.
Q. Who else?
A. There was Jasper who went out; there were three or four who went out.
Q. There were three or four men who went out?
Q. Who were they?
A. There was Dave, he went out afterwards, and Jasper went out.
Q. How long after Honore went out did Jack Pierre go out?
A. He left nearly fifteen or twenty minutes before they came back.
Q. Both Honore and Jack Pierre were out of the house?
A. Yes sir.
Q. What they did, you don't know?
Q. You don't know who threw the missile?
A. No sir.
Q. You don't know anything about the cutting of this man Sherman?
A. No sir.[171]

This district attorney, Parker questioned Davis about the whereabouts of Jack Pierre. Davis said Jack Pierre was outside fifteen minutes. Parker asked Davis if Pierre seem agitated.

Q. When he returned did Pierre seem agitated?
A. Yes sir.
Q. Excited?
A. Yes sir.

---

[170] Ibid., p. 65.
[171] Ibid., p. 68.

Q. Now you said you didn't know when the officer came?
A. No sir.
Q. You cannot say that Pierre was not out in the yard at the time he was killed?
A. No sir.
Q. He may have been?
A. Yes sir.
Q. Where was Father Abraham, was he in the room?
A. No sir, he was in the yard.
Q. When this trouble occurred you didn't pay much attention to it except to send a member out?
A. Yes sir.[172]

This ended of Sam Davis's testimony. The next witness was Jack Pierre, who testified on his own behalf. Luzenberg asked Jack Pierre questions concerning the night Cambias was killed. He asked Pierre if he knew Bertonnierre and he responded that he knew him about twelve years. Pierre gave his own version of happened the night of the incident.

Q. You were arrested and charged with the murder at the same time that the other men were, and you were taken to the lower court, and you pleaded not guilty, and there Honore and yourself was indicted by the Grand Jury?
A. Yes sir.
Q. Now on the night of the 18th of October did you attend this meeting?
A. Yes sir.
Q. Of the Council of God?
A. Yes sir.
Q. Why did you go there?
A. I was in the habit of going to the meeting to hear the lecture or Ten Commandments.
Q. Did you go armed or did you carry any weapons?
A. The Ten Commandments show you how to live in righteousness.
Q. At the time of the meeting did any one throw any stones?
A. Yes sir, they were throwing stones at the building.[173]

---

172 Ibid., p. 70.
173 Ibid., p. 71.

Luzenberg questioned Pierre about Honore and who went out to stop the stone throwing.

> Q. Who did it; did anyone tell anyone to go out and to put a stop to it?
> A. Davis told Honore to stop it.
> Q. Did Honore go out?
> A. He went out, and Latimore went out, Jasper, Boyd and I went out.
> Q. Who was the last man?
> A. Dave Majors.
> Q. After you went out tell the jury what happen?
> A. I went out and stopped in the gate, and the other fellows they went around, and at this time this little boy, John Sherman, I said to him what do you mean, and he said what do you reckon I meant and I said someone ought to beat the devil out of you, he made a swipe and I took this away from him.
> Q. Did you cut his hand?
> A. At this time when I did that Ferdinand Boyd he came out and they ran him.[174]

Jack Pierre then gave his version of the incident.

> Q. That is the truth?
> A. Yes sir.
> Q. How long after that did you stay in the yard?
> A. I was in the yard about five minutes and then I went inside.
> Q. Did the others?
> A. No sir, I never seen them.
> Q. You are pretty badly frightened are you nervous?
> A. No sir.
> Q. How long did you stay in this hall before you went out?
> A. I believe about half an hour.
> Q. Did you go out again?
> A. I heard them call him.
> Q. What did you hear them call?
> A. Latimore called me.
> Q. What happened then?
> A. I saw the officer.
> Q. Was Honore there?
> A. Yes sir.
> Q. What was Honore doing?
> A. The officer said that he was going to place Honore under arrest.
> Q. Was Latimore and Boyd there?

---

[174] Ibid., p. 72.

A. Yes sir.

Q. He said he was going to place him under arrest? Then what happened?

A. Then I walked this way, Latimore when he got to the gate, Latimore told Honore not to go, and the officer did like this, and this fellow Honore grabbed him, and grabbed the revolver out of his hand, and then I seen Honore jump on him and Ferdinand Boyd and Latimore.

Q. Where were you standing?

A. Right by the stable.

Q. Did they shove him out and jump on him?

A. Yes sir, this little boy Sherman was standing up like that when they shoved him out of the door.

Q. After he was out they jumped on him?

A. Well, I never noticed who was on the right side; I know Honore, Latimore and Ferdinand Boyd.

Q. You were scared? It happened quickly?

A. It didn't take a minute as soon as they shoved him out of the door they jumped on him.

Q. What did you do, did you stay around there?

A. I stayed around there until we went in.

Q. Did you speak to them?

A. No sir, I never said a word.

Q. That is the truth?

A. Yes sir.

Q. If at anytime you touched this officer I want you to tell the jury how you came to do it?

A. I never touched the officer. This boy Sherman seen I never touched the officer.

Q. You are on trial for the murder of this officer and these gentlemen are going to judge you, if at anytime you owned this razor, or any other I want you to tell the jury.

A. I never owned it.[175]

Luzenberg questioned Pierre his relationship with Dave Majors. Pierre maintained that Majors was frightened because he was in jail and would say anything to get out. Pierre also stated that Majors had lived with him at one

---

[175] Ibid., p. 73-74.

time, but he had put him out and as a result. Majors did not have any use for him. He, Pierre, continued to insist that he never held of the officer.[176]

The cross-examination of Pierre by Parker is the next line of questioning. Pierre was asked about seeing Sherman the night of the incident, and he responded that he did not observe the boy throwing at the house. Pierre stated he took a knife away from John Sherman. Pierre admitted that he exclaimed Sherman should be beaten, but insisted he never laid hands on him. Pierre stated that Sherman was with the officer when he came to the house and that he did not resist t he officer when Sherman pointed him out. He also maintained that he never left the yard and that he did not mention what happened to the high priest Davis. He further testified that he did not have the dirk and that he did not observe Honore with a dirk. He was asked about being in prison before and he admitted that he had been arrested for fighting but pointed out that he paid the fine.[177] Despite his protestation the jury found Pierre guilty of murder. He appealed his case to the Louisiana Supreme Court.

---

[176] Ibid., p. 74.
[177] Ibid., p. 74-78.

The Appeal

No.17065
Supreme Court of the State of Louisiana

State of Louisiana
Vs.
Jack Pierre

Opinion and Judgment Nicholls
Assigned and filed May 11th 1908 F. M. Haymans Clerk

Appeal from the Criminal District Court for the Parish of Orleans.
State of the Crime.

The defendant indicted for murder, was found guilty of the crime and was sentenced to death. He has appealed. He relies for reversal, upon a motion to squash the indictment on the grounds that follow:

1st. The Grand Jury finding the indictment in this case, was illegally constituted in this, to wit: that said Grand Jury was drawn by an unconstitutional body of Jury commissioners having been appointed by the Governor of this state; that the governor is without authority to appoint Jury commissioners, it having been decided by the supreme court of this state that the appointment of Jury Commissioners is a judicial, not on executive function.

The court over ruled the motion, and then ruling it is contended, was erroneous and entitles the defendant to a reversal of the judgment.

The court committed no error in overruling the motion. The appointment of Jury Commissioners by the Governor was made under Act no.98 of 1880, as amended by Act. No. 170 of 1894. Jury Commissioners are officers created by stature.

Act 71 of the constitution of 1888, referring to the Governor, declares: He shall nominate and by and with the consent of the senate appoint all officers whose offices are established by this constitution and whose appointment or elections one not herein otherwise provided for; provided that the General Assembly shall have the right to prescribe the mode of appointment or election to all officers created by it.[178] This was quoted from Pierre Appeal to the Louisiana Supreme Court.

The Governor making appointments of Jury Commissioners, acted under authority conferred on him by law and in so doing exercised executive functions. The fact that the officers whom he appointed maybe called on to perform duties connected with the judicial department does not make his act in appointing them in judicial act.

We are not now dealing with an act of the General Assembly authorizing or directing judges to appoint Jury Commissioners. The defendant's attorney complained on the grounds that such duty thrown on courts is in contravention of Article 96 of the Constitution. That question isn't entirely distinct from the one submitted to us.

We find no legal ground for a reversal of the judgment appealed from. It is therefore affirmed.

The syllabus written by Judge Nicholls was as follows:
1. Under Act No. 98 of 1880 and amended by Act No. 170 of 1894, the duty of appointing Jury Commissioners is vested in the Governor.
2. Jury Commissioners are statute officers and under Act 71 of the Constitution the General Assembly has the right to prescribe the mode of appointment to all offices created by it.

---

[178]State vs. Jack Pierre, Louisiana Supreme Court 1908, p. 1.

3. The Governor, making appointments to such offices under the authority conferred upon him so to do by the General Assembly, performs on executive function. The fact that an officer so appointed by him will have to perform judicial duties does not make the Governor's act in appointing him a judicial act.[179]

The Louisiana Supreme Court upheld the lower court decision and the sentence against Jack Pierre stood. Both men, Jack Pierre and Edward Honore were sentenced to be hanged for the murder of officer Cambias. The next and final chapter will deal with the hanging and it will include my conclusions. My thesis is that the murder of Robert Cambias was an act of self-defense by Edward Honore, and also that Jack Pierre was innocent of any involvement in the death of Robert Cambias. My contention is that the testimony of all of the witnesses was contradictory.

---

[179]Ibid., p. 2.

Chapter V

The Hanging and Conclusion

The trial of Jack Pierre ended and both he and Honore were sentenced to death by hanging. They had fought the good fight, and they lost the battle. Those bent on destroying the movement called The Council of God were victorious. The two defendants were not presumed innocent until found guilty, instead, they were declared guilty by the public and the law. The jury was not composed of their peers and they lacked the means to procure a lawyer that would fight for them all the way to the Supreme Court. Thus they now awaited the date of their execution.

> On March 21, 1908 after all arguments were heard, Judge Chretin ordered Pierre to rise and state any reason why the sentence of the law should not be pronounced against him. The Prophet Ezekiel accepted the edict calmly and delivered an address to the court in which he proclaimed that death had no terror for him, for he was certain of returning to earth again."[180]

Jack Pierre made remarks about the Bible that observers believed were weird and uncanny. He spoke at length both on the Lord, and the unfairness of his trial. In this regard he insisted that the witnesses against him were unfair and not truthful. He further claimed that he was well acquainted with God and was ready to face him. The judge countered saying that Pierre was adequately represented and that his trial was fair. The judge then ruled that he would be

---

[180] W. P. A. Dillon. (Northwestern State University Watson Memorial Library), (Cammie G. Henry Research Center) Folder 91 p. 40

hanged by the neck whenever the Governor ordered the time.[181]   Honore

accepted his sentence without protest. The double hanging was set for October

23, 1908.

The day before the final hours of life was passed by the prisoners talking

to family members. The two men who were about to be hung passed the day

without much concern for the day of their death.

> On the eve of their executions although Pierre and Honore were
> fanatically inclined to believe that they were victims of the white man's
> hatred, they were composed and ate with relish. Final farewells were
> taken without tears, the wives of the men seemed the least affected.[182]

The date of the hanging was greeted by the two men, Honore and Pierre,

without remorse. There were no religious ceremonies. Jack Pierre followed his

usual practice and read the Bible. Pierre and Honore refused to accept the

consolation of a Dominican Priest.   Pierre informed the priest that he had

committed no crime and he was content in his beliefs. He insisted that the father

of all was waiting to receive him.   Both men believed that they would be

reincarnated and would return to earth as men of affluence and ease.[183]   Pierre

stated, "I am prepared to go anytime, I am innocent of the crime charged against

me, and it is unjust that I should go that way, but the Lords will be done."[184]

Pierre had a talent for drawing and depicted Bible symbols on a handkerchief.

He drew the images with crayons provided by Sheriff Long.   Some of the

characters on the handkerchiefs were, the Horn of Gabriel, The Keys of Heaven,

---

[181] Ibid.,,. p. 40
[182] Ibid.,,. p.40
[183] Ibid.,,. p. 43
[184] Daily Picayune, Sept. 17, 1908 p.95 C 2-3

The Rock of Ages and The Rod of Aaron. He gave his daughter a handkerchief that he spent extra effort on. This was his way to say goodbye to his youngest daughter. Pierre gave handkerchiefs to his jailers, including the sheriff and certain deputies.[185]

There was a large crowd of whites who assembled to see the two men hang for the death of Robert Cambias. Most of the crowd came to see the black men who they believed had committed the worst crime in New Orleans police history punished. They also came because it was the first double hanging in a quarter century.[186]

The atmosphere was festive as spectators swarmed about the prison. Some were prompted by morbid curiosity. Many came to see men they considered fanatics, pay for their killing of a fellow white, who was a policeman, with their own lives. The incident was also considered by some as a warning to other Negroes who were members of the Counsel of God. They also came to see the Negroes pay for their inferior beliefs and belligerent attitude towards whites and to cease spreading discontent among their race under the guise of Biblical characters.[187] This is the way James Dillion describes the hanging. He had the assistance of the Daily Picayune, which had at the time of the incident created a biased image of these two black men.

Pierre also left a final letter he wrote to be published in the newspapers. This letter sounds like something Jesus, would have left to the Romans. Pierre

---

[185] Ibid., October 23, 1908, p. 5 C-1
[186] Dillon, The Council of God, p.44
[187] Ibid.

worked for a week on his farewell address to the world. The letter was incoherent and lengthy. The letter reads as follows:

> Last letter and goodbye by the prophet Ezekiel Jack Pierre, God's own prophet. Brother men and sisters: I leave this world of wonder to enter my father's house to roam no more, and be at rest. I would have you know that God made all things and without him not anything was made. And this is the truth. And brother men and sisters, I would have you know that some of the Council of God enemies say that the Council of God does not believe in God. But I say unto you, that is not true. Brothers we wouldn't confess to the priest, because God know all things and he made all things according to his own image and likeness thereof, and made all men and blessed the good ones and I being the Holy Prophet of God being so sanctified and glorified in the wisdom and understanding of the works of God to teach man the truth. Let man hear. He that hath ears to hear, let him hear. Judge not, least ye be judged as the people judge, the Council of God knows that I am innocent of the deeds that the people have charged me with; he knows how false witnesses have sworn against me to destroy my presence from the face of the earth, but he knows that my soul shall dwell with my father which art in heaven and if I am wrong my father will condemn me to everlasting punishment for ever. For he is a just God. Peace be onto these.[188]

The day of the hanging Pierre accused Honore of giving false testimony. "I am the Prophet of God and I die innocent," he said, "I go to meet my death because of false witnesses. My brother here on the left would not give the true statement. Had he given the true statement, I would not be here today. Now you say something."[189]

Pierre was calm, but according to the witness Honore was visibly nervous. Honore stated that Pierre was behind him when the policeman was killed. Honore stated that he did not kill the officer. He, Honore, stated that it was not

---

[188] Daily Picayune 5, C-1
[189] W. P. A. Dillon p. 44

94

true that Pierre held the officer.[190] This was stated by Honore after the sentencing was announced.

When the time came Pierre and Honore walked calmly to the gallows. The black cap was placed over Pierre's head as he called a smothered goodbye to the crowd, and the hangman was busy doing his work. The noose was placed under the left side of Pierre's jaw a position that hindered a quick death. The black cap was placed over Honore head and the hangman's noose was drawn under his left jaw and in a position near his left ear, which made his death sudden. The time of the hanging was 12:44 pm when Johnston the hangman cut the rope holding the trap door. The doors opened and the two men plunged downwards to their death. Honore gave a sound of smothering when the fall suddenly stopped, his struggle was brief. This was not the case with Pierre.[191]

Honore was dead without a struggle. His body hung motionless at the end of the gently swaying rope, and there was no sign of nervous twitching in his dangling body. Pierre's death was different. Honore was dead from a broken neck. Pierre died slowly from strangulation. His end created a horrible scene. His shoulders rose and fell, his back twisted and the right wrist struggled desperately in the upward jerking of the arm evidently in an effort to be free of the rope which bound it. Pierre's struggle lasted for fifteen minutes, and after his body ceased to move, it was noted that his fingernails had cut deeply into his hands. The crowd watched the struggle with various emotions.[192]

---

[190] Ibid.
[191] Daily Picayune October 24, 1908. p.5
[192] Ibid., p. 5

95

At 12:36 Honore's body was laid out on one of the morgue tables after having hung for twenty-two minutes. At 12:42 Pierre was lowered after he had been hanging for twenty-eight minutes. Pierre's face showed signs of a man who had died in awful pain. His eyes were running water, and a thick froth smeared his goatee.[193]

Conclusion

The incident of October 19, 1907 in New Orleans involving a policeman and the Council of God was regarded as the act of fanatics. The main thesis of this paper is that the two men hanged for the murder of Officer Cambias were innocent.

This was not an incident of murder, but was the act of a man reacting in self-defense to the action of a policeman. This was the act of Edward Honore, who was put to death by the justice system in New Orleans. Jack Pierre appeared to be a victim of circumstances over which he had no control. The Daily Picayune contribute to a public bias against Honore and Pierre before the trial. The two men were condemned to die by the pen of newspapermen who acted as judge and jury. During the trial the Daily Picayune published inflammatory material. A cartoon depicting the Counsel of God published by this paper is including in the illustration. Moreover the defense attorney Luzenberg effectively question the legality of the jury commission appointed by the governor. In addition the jury was not composed of Pierre and Honore's peers and their

---

[193] Ibid., p. 5 C-1

96

was no defense counsel provided for the accused during the indictment phase of the trial.

The trial of Honore was brief lasting only a few hours. In this trial the chief witness stated that the police officer pointed and snapped his gun at the defendant. Honore testified that he had slashed the officer because of this. The testimony of the witness, Bertonnierre, was questionable. He admitted he had done nothing to stop the killing. He stated that he was on a step near the gate where the boy Sherman ran a few feet away and he did not see him. He did nothing to stop the killing. Honore did not deny that he cut the officer, admitting that he used a razor on him. But, the coroner testified that the razor cut was not fatal, but that a stab wound caused by a pointed weapon was the cause of death. The murder weapon, identified as a dirk, was not Honore's. It was established in the trial that Latimore Boyd had had the weapon in his possession before the incident.

The trial of Jack Pierre was drawn out and lengthy. It lasted longer than Honore's trial. Unlike Honore, Pierre had a lawyer that tried to save his life. Luzenberg did what he thought was correct in the case, but the judge who was over the trial did not give Pierre the benefit of doubt. Nevertheless, Luzenberg created grounds for reasonable doubt. The witness Henry Boyd, alias Father Abraham, stated he did not see Jack Pierre do anything. Jack Pierre protested that he did not kill the officer. Sam Davis, alias, the high Priest, also testified that Pierre was on the inside when the officer was killed. The defense maintained that Pierre could not have stabbed Cambias, since he was unaware of the dirk. But because of the existed bias disclaimed by Luzenberg was unsuccessful and Pierre was convicted.

In the trial of Jack Pierre it was shown that the testimony of the witnesses Henry Boyd and Dave Majors was that of lunatics out of their minds. Boyd and Majors testified that they had occupied multiple bodies since the foundation of the world. Boyd said that he was the same Abraham that existed thousands of years before in Biblical times. Even though the sanity of the key witness mind was questionable, the judge did not have them examined by an expert.

To the author of this study, the innocence of Pierre is quite evident and he agrees with the protestations of Pierre that he was being put to death wrongly.

The incident of October 19, 1907 in New Orleans involving the Council of God ended in a hanging. These men Honore and Pierre were men who thought for themselves. They refused to accept the Catholic Priest offer to confess to him, thereby rejecting the religious conception of Catholicism. These men were not murderers; it was a case of self-defense and being in the wrong circumstances. They were simply not guilty.

Bibliography

Secondary Sources

Baer, Hans A., <u>The Black Spiritual Movement a Religious Response to Racism</u>. Knoxville: University of Tennessee Press, 1984.

Billingsley, Andrew, <u>Mighty Like a River</u>. New York: Oxford University Press, 1999.

Blassingame, John W., <u>The Slave Community</u>. New York: Oxford University Press, 1972.

Blassingame, John W., <u>Black New Orleans</u>. Chicago: University of Chicago Press, 1973.

Bracey, Jr., August, Meier, and Rudwick Elliott, Ed, <u>Black Nationalism in America</u>. New York: Bobbs-Merril Company Inc., 1970.

Cell, John W., <u>The Highest Stage of White Supremacy</u>. Cambridge: Cambridge University Press, 1982.

Childs, John Brown, <u>The Political Black Minister</u>. Boston: G.K. Hall and Co., 1980.

Dubois, W.E.B., <u>The Souls of Black Folk</u>. Chicago: A.C. Mclurg and Co., 1903.

Hair, William Ivy, <u>Bourbonism and Agarian Protest</u>. Baton Rouge: Louisiana State University Press, 1969.

Hair, William Ivy, <u>Carnival of Fury</u>. Baton Rouge: Louisiana State University Press, 1976.

Jackson, Joy J., <u>New Orleans in the Gilded Age</u>. Baton Rouge: Louisiana State University Press, 1969

Kemp, James R., <u>Martin Behrman of New Orleans</u>. Baton Rouge: Louisiana State University Press, 1977.

Kousser, J. Morgan, <u>The Shaping of Southern Politics</u>. New Haven: Yale University Press, 1974

Painter, Nell Irvin, <u>Exodusters</u> Lawrence: University Press of Kansas, 1976

Serneth, Milton, <u>Afro-American Religion</u>.
   Durham: Duke University Press, 1985.

Stuckey, Sterling, <u>Slave Culture</u>.
   New York: Oxford University Press, 1987.

Twombly, Robert C., <u>Blacks in White America</u>.
   New York: David McKay Company, Inc., 1971.

Woodard, C. Vann, <u>The Burden of Southern History</u>.
   Baton Rouge: Louisiana State University Press, 1960.

Primary Sources

Daily Picayune, 31 October 1907-19 October 1908.

Times Democrate, 31 October 1907-19 October 1908.

State of Louisiana US. Edward Honore, Docket No. 17,065. Louisiana Supreme Court. (March 23, 1908).

State of Louisiana US. Edward Honore, Docket No. 38,812 Criminal District Court Parish of Orleans Sec. B. (February 5, 1908).

State of Louisiana V. Jack Pierre Supreme Court of Louisiana No. 17065 April 14, 1908.

State of Louisiana V. Jack Pierre, Criminal District Court, Sec. B. Parish of Orleans (December 12, 1907).

W.P.A. Dillon (Natchitoches: Northwestern State University of Louisiana, Watson Memorial Library, Cammie G. Henry Research Center) Folder 91 (1 of 3).

Printed in the United States
By Bookmasters